W9-CON-789

Social and Cultural Change

Challenge and Change for the Military

Social and Cultural Change

Edited by David Last, Franklin Pinch,
Douglas L. Bland, Alan Okros

Published for the School of Policy Studies, Queen's University and
The Canadian Forces Leadership Institute
by McGill-Queen's University Press
Montreal & Kingston • London • Ithaca

National Library of Canada Cataloguing in Publication

Social and cultural change / edited by David Last ... [et al.].

(Challenge and change for the military)
This book brings together papers developed from the conference
"Challenge and Change for the Military, Institution and Profession", held in
Kingston in October, 2002.
Includes bibliographical references.
ISBN 1-55339-033-4 (bound).—ISBN 1-55339-032-6 (pbk.)

1. Sociology, Military—Congresses. I. Last, David M. II. Queen's
University. School of Policy Studies. III. Canadian Forces Leadership
Institute. IV. Challenge and Change for the Military, Institution and
Profession (2002 : Kingston, Ont.) V. Series.

U21.5.S63 2004   306.2'7   C2004-901768-3

Contents

Foreword
The Challenge of Social and Cultural Change

Rear Admiral David Morse, CMM, CD
Commander, Canadian Defence Academy

Social and cultural change in a shrinking world are our common professional challenge, and countries that are neither superpowers nor dependencies have much to learn from each other. It is a professional challenge that can be met through military education resting on focussed research like the work in this volume.

The Cold War isolated military professionals from society. Concepts of mutually assured destruction and deterrence were difficult to put into plain language and demanded highly specialized military skills that had no utility or parallel in Canadian society. Furthermore, European basing removed large parts of the Canadian military from contact with the homeland. Then the world changed. The fall of the Berlin Wall changed the scope and focus of missions and unleashed societal change. One can argue that the trends towards greater utility, accountability, and transparency are driven, at least in part, by the events of 1989.

We in the Canadian Forces tried to respond to the new world using old paradigms – models of professionalism, force structure and organization, mobility and capability that simply did not work. Nowhere was this more evident than in our experience in Somalia. That deployment and its agonizing aftermath of self-examination left us all at sea. We did not find our old self-image in this new post-Cold War world, and we were not alone. For different but related reasons, politicians, police forces, teachers, and even lawyers have all faced new demands on their professionalism. To varying degrees, each profession is being forced to reinvent itself to face new challenges.

For the military, remaking ourselves has been far from easy. Reform demands dialogue with society. It demands leadership both in society, and in the military – providing external support for internal transformation.[1] It requires an intellectual *largesse d'esprit* and a willingness to invest in institutions to permit change. This is where books like this, and the conference from which it sprang, fit in. As professionals, we cannot afford to define our field narrowly to include only combat between organized armies. Our field is not limited to new wars, but embraces the new social conditions that precipitate them, and the changing cultures and values that condition our society's expectation of its professionals.

Andrew Gordon, in his masterful analysis of Jutland, described the Royal Navy of the First World War: "In the British Navy... the capacity to think was a handicap and an independent thinker or critical mind was a definite disability...In such cases serious thinking may be more dangerous than secret drinking." Can anyone doubt that the past two decades have been as tough on the Canadian Forces as the failure at Jutland was on the Royal Navy, and can we doubt that the secret to future success lies in developing the attributes that Gordon found lacking?

Let me paint a picture of the post-Cold War Canadian forces and the events that precipitated the fundamental reform of the profession and of professional development that is now underway. While I address only the Canadian experience, I suggest that it is relevant for other countries. As in other forces, the dramatic strategic changes and the desire for the ever-elusive peace dividend forced drastic structural change. We associate this with the loss of historical regiments, the closure of bases, the imposition of public sector management rules, the loss of core capabilities, and forced retirements. But beyond all this, I would point to the collapse of professional confidence. Structural changes and strategic uncertainty were the background to the Canadian leadership failures in Somalia. The initially tepid military response to those failures led to a collapse of professional identity and inevitably to doubts about our military ethos and the reliability of Canadian Forces leadership.

The daily headlines didn't help: "Secrecy Plagues Canada's Military"; "New Scandal Rocks Forces"; and "Somalia Panel Urges Purge of Top Brass". Outside experts, disaffected retirees, voices of genuine concern, and blatant sensationalism were indistinguishably mixed, obscuring reality. *They* became the enemy, and we seemed to lack the confidence and the means to reply to them. Other tangible issues weakened our sense of professional worth. A pay freeze seemed unequally applied to the military. Capital programs were cancelled, and we struggled on with outdated equipment, facing relentless demands for more operational capacity. There was a distinct feeling that the military was a failed institution, and each member was left alone to cope with the lack of public confidence. We became increasingly defensive and isolated from Canadian society. Only a very public campaign to address quality-of-life issues restored a measure of trust between leaders and the led. Today a growing chorus is calling for action to address the need for modern operational tools.

If this were not enough, the demise of the Cold War not only increased the operational tempo, but dramatically changed the skills required. The American experience in Somalia highlighted this, and it is relevant for any country engaged in the new environment. To quote General Krulak of the US Marine Corps:

> The inescapable lesson of Somalia...is that outcome [of a mission] may hinge on decisions made by small unit leaders and by actions taken at the *lowest* level...Today's marines will often operate 'far from the flagpole' without the direct supervision of senior leadership...In order to succeed...[the marine] will require unwavering maturity, judgement, and strength of character...These missions will require...well-reasoned and independent decisions...He will become the strategic corporal.[2]

As Canadians we have a new sense of inclusion – found not only in combat operations responding to the universal revulsion against ethnic cleansing in the Balkans and terrorism in the Middle East, but also in direct support to the Canadian population – the crises of ice storms and floods. All these operations have demanded a military response, and every military member has responded. The Canadian public has noticed, giving us a new sense of confidence that we have the abilities that Canadians need, want, and value. Eleven thousand recruits this past year reinforce the impression that young Canadians still have a motivation to serve.

In 1997, Canadian Minister of National Defence Doug Young responded to the Somalia inquiry (and anticipated the "strategic corporal") by submitting a report to the Prime Minister on *Leadership and Management in the Canadian Forces*. From this direct ministerial intervention, we have redefined and reaffirmed the profession of arms in Canada and have embarked on a broad program of change in professional development. This redefinition begins with the insistence that military service is an honourable profession and that it must be led from within. To paraphrase the opening of *The Profession of Arms* manual:

> The Canadian Forces' functional imperative is to conduct military operations. This operational imperative shapes the fighting identity of Canada's military professionals; delineates the responsibility of the profession to the government and to society; and dictates the expertise that is necessary for the successful conduct of operations. The military ethos is derived from the Canadian Forces' unique role and responsibilities within Canadian society.

To summarize the starting point for *The Profession of Arms* Manual, modern operations demand broader theoretical and practical expertise from all ranks. Canadians demand that their military stand as exemplars of national values. Legitimacy and the wide scope afforded the profession to regulate itself are critically dependent on an appropriate ethos and its coherent and consistent practice in shaping and guiding conduct, especially in the face of ethical dilemmas. Social and cultural changes throw those ethical dilemmas into stark relief, as this volume demonstrates.

NOTES

1. Remarks of the Minister of National Defence at the Toronto Board of Trade, 25 October 2002.
2. General Charles C. Krulak, "The Strategic Corporal: Leadership in the Three Block War," Marines Magazine, January 1999.

Acknowledgements

In October 2002, the Inter-University Seminar on Armed Forces and Society (IUS): Canada Region, in cooperation with the Canadian Forces Leadership Institute and the Queen's University Defence Management Studies Program, co-sponsored an international conference in Kingston, Ontario. This project is the result of IUS Canada's first international conference and, most especially, the work of those scholars who participated and agreed to have their work published.

IUS Canada is a regional organization within the IUS International that was founded by the noted military sociologist, Morris Janowitz, at the University of Chicago in the 1960s. It is dedicated to independent social science research and scholarship that focus both on the relationship between the military and society and on the military institution itself. The Fellows of the IUS, numbering more than 800, represent a broad range of disciplines and some 50 countries, and are involved in the study of armed forces and society within academic institutions, research establishments and military forces around the world. The President at the time of the conference was Dr. David R. Segal, Distinguished Professor of Sociology at the University of Maryland. IUS Canada was established in 1981, and the current Chair is Dr. Franklin C. Pinch, Senior Research Fellow at the Canadian Forces Leadership Institute, Kingston, Ontario. Lieutenant Colonel (Dr.) David Last is the Kingston Area IUS Coordinator and was Program Chair of IUS Canada Conference.

The Canadian Forces Leadership Institute was established in 2001, with a broad mandate for leadership concept development, leadership research and cooperation with academic institutions and international research associations; it is directed by Captain (Navy) Alan Okros. The Queen's University Defence Management

Studies Program (DMSP) is one of 16 university chairs sponsored by the Department of National Defence's Security and Defence Forum (SDF). Dr. Douglas Bland has been Chair of DMSP since its inception in 1996.

We wish to express our sincere gratitude to all those who assisted in making the IUS Canada Conference 2002 a success. These include Lois Jordan, Conference Coordinator, and her most able assistants, Francine Allard and Joanne Thurlbeck for a superb "front desk" operation, and those who worked behind the scenes, including Jamie Green, Aimee MacDonald, and Brigitte Conrad-Avarma for ensuring that the web site was up and running and that our other technological needs were fulfilled. Finally, we appreciate the support we received from David Segal, IUS President, and E.L. "Doc" Hunter, Manager, IUS Secretariat.

The institutional support of the Royal Military College of Canada, the Canadian Forces Leadership Institute, the Queen's University Defence Management Studies Program, and the Canadian Defence Academy have made it possible to complete this volume. Trisha Mitchell and Joanne Simms in particular have provided capable administrative support. Moira Jackson's able editing and perceptive comments have been much appreciated. Mark Howes and Valerie Jarus at the School of Policy Studies Publications Unit, Queen's University, are thanked for their patience, professionalism, and hard work.

one

Introduction
Challenge and Change for the Military

David Last

This book brings together papers developed from the conference "Challenge and Change for the Military, Institution and Profession", held in Kingston in October 2002. It is about
the interaction of social and cultural change and new operations,
and it draws on the research skills and expertise of practical military men and women and of academics who are members of the
Inter-University Seminar on Armed Forces and Society (IUS).

A lifetime of experience cannot prepare military leaders for
the new types of operations already evident around us. Not only
are military operations changing, but the culture and values of
military institutions are changing. If they understand and manage the change well, leaders might be able to use the social and
cultural changes in institutions to conduct operations more effectively. Successful leaders in the future will be the ones who think
through their new tasks sufficiently clearly to take advantage of
social and cultural change. Changes affect the military job to be
done, the capability of military personnel to do it, and the way
society judges military performance. Our colleagues today are helping rebuild societies in Iraq and Afghanistan. Are they benefiting
from an understanding of Muslims' efforts to adjust to capitalism
and democracy in the West? Are the Western forces ready to accommodate Muslim differences and build them into cohesive teams
for international service?

Two varieties of military sociology are evident in IUS scholarship. Some work is essentially inward looking, considering the
social structures and relationships of military forces and military

personnel. Other work is outward looking, considering military forces and personnel as parts of a larger civilian society. This book contains both, but is primarily outward looking, drawing on international work in several disciplines for insights that cross cultural boundaries and inform both soldiers and society about their relationships.

The book is in two parts. In the first part, authors examine new types of operations that demand a more subtle understanding of social and cultural variables, because these variables themselves may be the centre of gravity for the operation. In the second part, authors consider the changing culture and values that constitute the shifting ground on which today's armed forces must operate. The volume should be a useful resource for soldiers or civilians contemplating the social and cultural changes that affect military leaders and their response to today's operational challenges.

PART I – CHANGING OPERATIONS

Thorsten Kodalle is part of the new generation of German military analysts confronting post-Cold War security problems for post-unification Germany – a country whose pivotal role in the new Europe brings threats and responsibilities. German thinking about security identifies political, economic, and social dimensions of future conflict. Kodalle describes how globalization marginalizes some actors while multipolarity empowers them. Against this background democratization is the most promising form of social and economic organization to manage change. For Kodalle, "small wars" are those that are waged neither between states nor across state boundaries, and constitute the most common form of organized violence. The German Defence Ministry concludes "security can no longer be seen as the preserve of one department...political, economic and social developments can all generate threats to security, requiring a holistic response." But this goes beyond more complex national configurations of joint and combined operations. "A coherent security policy to address the problems of small wars requires shaping the global community. The most developed states must assume their primary responsibility for civilisation and security". If this sounds imperialistic, it should be read with the accent on the word "community" – because democracy and an equitable economy in the global community are the vision of security that the German general staff seem to be advocating.

We would be wrong, however, to think that preserving order is a western prerogative. Every state, and many associations of states and non-state actors, strive to maintain order within their neighbourhoods and communities. India and Israel are two cases in point. Leena Parmar is an eminent Indian sociologist with long-standing connections to the Indian army, and personal knowledge of its complex operations in India's sensitive border regions. She describes the need to redefine security in economic and social terms in order to combat the disorder of sectarian demands. Achieving security may demand the non-traditional use of military forces. Parmar makes reference to India's parallels with Israel, and defines peace in terms of both physical and structural violence. I am intrigued by what appears to be institutional learning from international missions: "If Indian peacekeeping forces are dispatched to other countries around the world, General Ray asks, why can the Army not be used at home for peaceful nation-building?"

The importance of community-based development as a prerequisite for managing insurgency has been understood at least since the British counter-insurgency operations in Malaysia, but more sophisticated understanding of social and cultural dimensions might take us beyond the management of physical violence and yield new tools to manage the inherent structural violence of policing across cultural boundaries. Deborah Heifetz-Yahav recently completed three years of research and field observations of Israeli-Palestinian security cooperation. Her knowledge of theatre and dance as well as the language, culture, and anthropology of violence makes this an important contribution at two levels. She not only describes the unique institution of "non-mediated peacekeeping" (perhaps as dramatic as the unlikely prospect of British soldiers on joint patrols with the IRA), but describes the interpersonal performances that make it possible. I would invite the reader here to put aside the interminable complexities of the Middle East conflict and focus on what we can learn about one particular set of mechanisms to permit accommodation. Heifetz-Yahav's use of language – men and manning – is a reminder that notwithstanding our aspiration to be gender-neutral, masculinity is fundamental to understanding both violence and ways to manage it. The techniques of field observation that Heifetz-Yahav has used to describe non-mediated peacekeeping help to map the sort of network of relationships that Ulrich vom Hagen writes about as "social capital" in the second part of this book.

Tami Jacoby has also spent time studying conflict in the Middle East, but comes to the question of policing and security from a sociological perspective closer to Parmar's than to Heifetz-Yahav's. Drawing on interviews with government officials, Jacoby traces some of the convergence between police and military tasks. The link between policing and military security functions, within communities, states, and the larger international community, has always been closer than one might guess from the separate academic worlds that study them, and Jacoby's study suggests that closer cooperation and a blending of constabulary and coercive functions will be the norm in the future, for both domestic and international operations.

Three themes unite the four perspectives on changing operations, and relate them to the problem of social and cultural change. The first theme is power. Powerful actors seek to reduce threats to their power and positions of privilege. Thorsten Kodalle's chapter on small wars describes a world in which the developed, civilized nations have a responsibility for shaping an equitable world order that will reduce the incidence of small wars that threaten their interests. Leena Parmar describes the efforts of a powerful state to win over the marginalized communities on its borders in order to reduce incursions. Deborah Heifetz-Yahav describes the asymmetry between Israeli and Palestinian police – although power clearly rests with the Israelis, the Palestinians force local conformity to their own standards of behaviour. Jacoby argues for a rethinking of the balance between the coercive powers of the military and the social support and public respect required for policing – but also for counter-terrorism and homeland defence.

The second theme is convergence. The demands of negative peace (the absence of physical violence) are converging with the demands of positive peace (the absence of structural violence) or the presence of equitable social, economic, and political development. All four authors argue for the interconnectedness of security in the political, social, and economic spheres. For Kodalle, this means a coherent strategy at the international level. For Jacoby, it means closer collaboration between agencies at the national level. For Hiefetz-Yahav and Parmar, it means new kinds of operations carried out in the pursuit of elusive and sometimes illusory peace.

The third theme is adaptation. Each of the authors implies ways in which military organizations and the civilian agencies with which they work must adapt to new tasks and operational environments. For Kodalle, armies must adapt to denationalized wars that cut across economic and political boundaries. For Jacoby, armies and police forces have to find new ways of collaborating. For Parmar, military operations take on a social and economic character. For Heifetz-Yahav, soldiers and police must adapt to the alien culture with which cooperation is essential for success.

PART II – CHANGING CULTURE AND VALUES

Small wars, counter-terrorism, homeland security and internal peacekeeping operations would be challenging in a static environment, but the very developments that lead to them also change the societies trying to respond to them. The authors of the second part of the book provide concepts and methods that help us to understand culture and values, and map their contribution to the pursuit of security.

When we try to describe why a unit works well or not, how to build morale and group cohesion, or how networks of friends and colleagues like the "old boys' net" or regimental senates make things happen, we are playing with the concept of social capital. German military sociologist Ullrich vom Hagen writes, "...social capital plays a decisive role wherever social relations, social trust, solidarity, moral norms, or even the efficiency of administrative and political systems is in question..." Vom Hagen's work is important because he brings into the military context a debate that has influenced a lot of thinking about social capital in civic life. In the United States, social capital is conceived of mainly as a collective asset embracing trust, reciprocity, and engagement in civic associations. In Europe, it is often described as an individual resource, encompassing economic and cultural capital in ways that can undermine community by supporting the interests of elites. The literature on social capital to which vom Hagen points is an important tool for analyzing the ways in which military culture is changing, and has implications for each of the other chapters in this section.

Turkish researcher Gökhan Yücel's chapter on Turkey provides an instructive example of a national security culture clashing with changing social values. The central problem is that "...regime security seems to be synonymous with national security in the Turkish case. The national security syndrome therefore clashes with democratic culture." Economic and social problems, which foster secessionism and Islamic fundamentalism, can only be solved within a democratic culture that brings Turkey closer to European values. But this in turn makes military security against these threats more difficult to achieve. Must the military guardians of national security and their political allies adjust their values in order to avoid a "catch-22" in which the pursuit of security undermines it? The new emphasis on homeland security in Europe and North America puts us closer to this dilemma than some realize.

The powerful metaphors that we use to describe national security and the relationship of the armed forces to society may be more universal than the sophisticated concept of "social capital". Anthropologist Brian Selmeski describes how the family metaphor helps build national cohesion amongst Ecuadorian conscripts: "...the family model illuminates and shapes the armed forces' relationship with other segments of society...Unlike the adversarial relationship of the health metaphor, where 'physicians' (soldiers) had to 'cut out' (kill or disappear) 'cancerous cells' (dissidents) so that the organism (State) could thrive, the Ecuadorian model produces social consensus..." His fascinating first-hand account is more than a good story; it illustrates how anthropology contributes to our understanding of military interaction with society and suggests new work waiting to be done in other countries.

Another eminent anthropologist, Donna Winslow, has written on Canadian military culture but turns her attention here to the coalescing European military institution, EUROMIL – the European Organization of Military Associations. Many people see the building of security and defence values that transcend national boundaries as a logical and necessary extension of European integration. But there are nationalist forces that resist it, just as the national security paradigm in Turkey resists European integration. Winslow writes: "EUROMIL tells us that the goals of unification, harmonization and integration, key processes in the context of Europe-building, require an alteration in the core areas that were previously defined within the frame of nation states. In particular, national defense policies and the determination of EU states to keep control over defense run counter to the fostering of common forms of EU identity and affiliation and may even subvert efforts to build a common European defense force." EUROMIL protests against differences in the political and social rights of soldiers in different European countries, "joint missions – joint rights". In so doing, it is working toward a conception of European citizenship, and citizens in uniform, who are prepared to defend human rights and the principle of liberty beyond national boundaries. It is a vision that is wholly congruent with the pursuit of democracy and rights as antidotes to small wars in a global community, suggested by Kodalle.

The themes of power, convergence, and adaptation are evident in these chapters, too. Vom Hagen helps us to understand social capital as a source of organizational power, in much the same way that economic capital is a source of economic power. EUROMIL can be seen as a new player with social capital on the European scene, and as a power-base for changing values in military institutions. The convergence of the requirements for avoiding violence and for making economic and social progress is particularly evident in Yücel's description of the dilemma facing Turkey. Not surprisingly, adaptation to changing values and cultural pressures is the dominant theme in these chapters. The competing concepts of social capital help us to understand adaptation by complex organizations. Turkey is struggling to adapt its national security culture to the demands of democracy, human rights, and economic integration with Europe. Ecuador has successfully adapted the metaphor of the family to serve the goal of national cohesion, and EUROMIL is forcing adaptation by armed forces and governments across Europe, and quite possibly making them stronger in the process.

Armed forces can no longer rely on rote indoctrination, but depend increasingly on professional education to adjust to changing values and prepare for complex new missions. The Principal of the Royal Military College of Canada, John Cowan, writes "...it may be that education and higher knowledge are the preventative for catastrophe, the soul of military renewal, and the final confirmation to the Canadian public that there is a genuine profession of arms in Canada." And this is a good note on which to conclude. If small wars need a global response, if officers must manage physical and structural violence that is inextricably linked, if values and culture are changing in ways that affect concepts of security, and if the military response must be integrated with political and social responses, then education is indeed the vital ground of the future.

Changing
Operations

two

The Security Challenge of Small Wars[1]

Thorsten Kodalle

The shocking events of 11 September 2001 showed the world how quickly and inhumanely violence can be brought to our own doorstep. The sense of privileged security in the West has given way to realization of vulnerability. Time will tell whether the war on terror can be won, or whether we face an age of new and different wars. But the terms "war" and "security" are being re-examined, which will shape both security policy and concepts for the evolution and employment of armed forces. This chapter analyzes the security challenges of the new century: small wars and the military response. What are the trends in conflict? How will they challenge today's military forces? What will these challenges mean for security policy and for modern armed forces?

The chapter draws on work at the Center for Analyses and Studies of the German Bundeswehr, conducted in January 2002, whose findings will also contribute to the study of future German security and defence policy known as SFT21.

The course of armed conflicts since the Second World War, no less than the attack on 11 September 2001, clearly shows that the modern pattern of war corresponds neither to the perceptions of the influential German thinker Carl von Clausewitz nor to the conditions of the Hague and Geneva Conventions. "Regulated" wars between states, such as the First and Second World Wars or the strategic nuclear exchange contemplated during the Cold War, appear to be exceptions in an era that has seen far more conflict within than between states. Even the conventional use of force in Afghanistan and Iraq calls for protracted policing commitments by Western powers. These new tasks for the armed forces undermine classical thinking and the notion of a separation between internal and external security. The challenges of the 21st century entail not only defence against threats but the development of a common world order that will help us cope with new forms of war and organized violence.

German thinking about security trends identifies patterns of economic, political, and social development that affect the emerging world order. Economic development is characterized by globalization. The transnational interconnection of systems, markets, and societies continues to advance. As the economic power of multinational enterprises grows, so, too, do their opportunities for exerting political influence. While globalization increases the prosperity of some, it aggravates the contrasts between rich and poor within and between nations and undermines social cohesion. "Losers" in the globalization process are marginalized not only within states but also at a regional and global level.

Political development is characterized by emerging multipolarity. The bipolar Cold War world gave way to American hegemony, but this is clearly challenged both by regional groups (though Europe was divided in its opposition to America's war in Iraq) and by non-state actors assuming influential geopolitical roles. Conflict-prone groups like Al-Quaeda do not strive to control government in the traditional sense. Ideology and religion, rather than international law, become the yardsticks for right and wrong, and the application of legal frameworks to both intrastate and international wars becomes difficult, if not impossible.

Non-state actors affecting international conflict include nongovernmental organizations, multinational enterprises, international terrorist networks, organized criminal syndicates, and ethnic and religious groups. The activities of these groups serve to undermine state authority and to erode governments' monopoly on the right to use force. Consequently, some states are unable to preserve public order, which further diminishes their legitimacy in the eyes of citizens. Fragmentation of the international system, the overwhelming power of the United States, and the influence of regional powers challenge the trend to multipolarity but do not stop it. The unilateral action of the United States in Iraq, for example, is offset by its need for allies in reconstruction. A multipolar world emphasizes the mutual dependence of economic, political, and social actors.

The trend of social development is toward democratization. The globalization of information and the dissemination of values suggest that the world will continue to become more open and market-oriented, and this trend promotes economic success.

Pluralism and free markets provide the basis for a continuing process of democratization. Since the end of the Cold War, liberal market democracies have proven universally to be the most promising form of social organization. A comparison of the economic productivities of societies clearly shows that the developed economies in the world are mainly found in democratic states. States striving for economic progress and a share of the growth in global prosperity will seek to organize as liberal democracies, if given the opportunity.

CHANGES IN SECURITY POLICY

Until the end of the Cold War, states were considered the only legitimate sources of violence, but since then there has been a tendency towards the privatization of war. Economic, political, and social dimensions of war will continue to precipitate large-scale displacements in many parts of the world. We would therefore expect more non-state actors, particularly in the form of warlords and mercenaries, to seek to further the interests of their clients by force. These actors have no interest in controlling or ending war because it becomes part of the fabric of their economic life. Many future conflicts, therefore, will see no clear separation between the use of force and conduct of business. We might even extrapolate this observation to include the conduct of the United States in Iraq, with ensuing reconstruction and development contracts for American-based enterprises. In general, however, the powerful global and regional poles of a new world order will not permit interstate wars, while resort to "small wars" within states may be part of a new political reality which threatens international stability.

A second form of conflict is "asymmetrical" threat that transcends national boundaries. Asymmetrical strategies gain advantage by using unconventional forms of attack on weak targets, such as terrorism to disrupt the economy, or biological weapons to demoralize the civilian population. Scientific and technical advances, including global communications, miniaturization, and the dissemination of scientific knowledge, increase the potential for asymmetric wars. They will become increasingly attractive because they can be waged easily and they allow the weak to attack the strong with little vulnerability. Exchanging violence for money is already popular, and it is encouraged by the growth of new criminal and ideologically inspired networks.

To understand the dangers that these networks pose to modern, technologically dependent societies, we need to look at how the borders of states and empires have changed over time. The German scholar Münkler argues that the majority of domestic wars have been waged along the "soft" borders of historic empires – the Austro-Hungarian Empire, the Ottoman Empire, Czarist Russia, the Soviet Union, and European colonial empires. Today, as a result of globalization, migration, and transnational non-state actors, the formerly "hard" national boundaries are becoming ever softer and more permeable. It is likely, therefore, that states hitherto relatively unaffected by domestic violence will find it increasing within their borders, spurred by international factors beyond their control. As a result, the boundary line between external and internal security will become less distinct.

As war becomes denationalized and integrated with economic life and the boundary between war and business becomes blurred, the use of force will become routine. Wherever local economies, political structures, and persuasive mechanisms decline (or are eroded by violent conflict), war will become a way of life. Violence will become the most important means of sustaining the livelihood of the new elite, who are recruited from the criminal elements at the fringes of society. Ravaging and plunder will take the place of production. In the absence of economic alternatives, there are incentives to continue the violence, and use of force becomes integrated into social life. It is difficult for fragmented warrior societies to return to civil society and democratic governance. The unification of social space and battlefield and the denationalization of war have consequences for international security.

The changing nature of war creates interdependent threats to security, which cannot be managed by military means alone but require interdepartmental and international efforts. If this were not complex enough, we can expect the number of relevant security actors to increase as technological breakthroughs and the dissemination of knowledge allow individuals, groups, and networks to control the means of violence.

SMALL WARS AND ARMED CONFLICTS

War is not a synonym for conflict, which may be a prerequisite for change and is often positive. Most conflicts are settled without violence. War is a specific way of settling conflict violently, usually between states, and is sometimes labelled "major armed conflict" or "large-scale military conflict". The emergence of states and their monopolization of violence after the Thirty Years' War reduced violence in Europe and permitted cultural and economic development. In the ensuing centuries, interstate war has been contained by practices amounting to an international law of armed conflict. In this framework, war can be characterized as organized combat conducted by opposing forces of similar strengths. Organization implies that two or more armed forces are involved, at least one of which represents a recognized government. It further implies that these forces are under some form of control and that operations are planned and authorized. War also implies duration, intensity, and continuity. Intensity can be measured by casualties and destruction. Continuity rules out unplanned, sporadic, or occasional inter-group violence. A war may be considered terminated when combat action ceases for more than a year.

Armed conflicts are violent disputes that do not meet all of the criteria for wars. This usually means that they lack the continuity or degree of organization to be considered wars. Terrorism might be seen as the most asymmetrical form of armed conflict, in which a comparatively weak non-state organization attacks the most vulnerable elements of a much stronger state. But counterterrorism efforts should not be labelled as wars, because this implies that appropriate means or responses are principally military.

Historically, the number of wars between states has decreased, but there has been no decline in the number of armed conflicts. We will use the term "small wars" to describe both armed conflicts and wars that are not waged between states. "Small wars" thus encompass large-scale armed and protracted violent conflicts between state and non-state actors, and among non-state actors. They may approach the violence of traditional interstate conflicts in violence and may surpass them in duration. Small wars reject rules and violate conventions. Many of the post-colonial states formed after 1945 have weak national institutions, and are victims of protracted civil wars, criminal regimes, and global social processes that undermine their sovereignty. In this environment, more and more non-state actors resort to organized force that transcends national boundaries. This threatens the process of civilizing and pacifying international politics.

What are the characteristics of the groups fighting these small wars? Their leaders often come from the urban middle or upper classes, including the national establishment. They have enjoyed a Western education, permitting them to communicate politically to the rest of the world. Their status is elevated by the "social honors" conferred by money, education, and birth. The supporting staff of such groups is composed mainly of specialists in violence drawn from groups with an appropriate professional ethic – not just military and police forces, but sometimes sports associations, clans, and tribes. The followers come from all parts of society, but particularly prominent are urban outlaws, the victims of war, refugees, and displaced populations. Rapid changes associated with modernization – urbanization, rural poverty, and the monetization of social relations – undermine the social institutions that help to regulate conflict. Frustrated expectations, fractionalization of society, and the destruction of institutions help to fuel recruitment to armed groups that promise wealth and power. The structures of the groups reflect their social origins and political contexts, reflecting the fight for power and influence within the group. Material reproduction of the groups fighting small wars may be based on resource extraction or any fungible asset (for example, timber in Malaysia and Indonesia, gemstones in Thailand and Sierra Leone, or coca in Colombia and Peru). Taxing migrants, international aid, and expatriate communities also help to support the fighting groups.

Small wars have characteristic impacts on economy, on ideology, and on international politics. No economic system is closed. Those benefiting from the fighting have an interest in continuing it. Even after the fighting stops, the problem of transforming combat-oriented groups into political actors and fighters into citizens has proven intractable. Internal conflicts between political and military actors favour hard-liners and make post-conflict politics unstable. Fighters hoping for better prospects may be frustrated and return to force of arms to earn a living, leading to widespread banditry; organized combat is replaced by high crime levels, as it was in Lebanon in the 1980s and in El Salvador and South Africa in the 1990s. Stabilization often requires a third-party presence. Thus postwar situations are often marked by the continuation of violence.

Civil wars may be part of the transition to stable statehood, but they can also become a permanent condition, shaping dangerous and violent societies. The convergence of business and armed violence is characteristic of small wars because funding is an important way in which they are differentiated from inter-state wars. Civil-war economies can transcend regions and intersect with the global economy. According to the World Bank, three quarters of the small wars waged by non-state actors in the past decade have had a principally economic rationale. Fighters serve themselves or a client community, and they do not feel bound by international law. Far from seeking to settle the conflict, the parties have an incentive to perpetuate it – war serves their economic interests better than peace. If official economies are unable to offer employment and satisfy human needs in the future, weak governing institutions will be unable to stop the spread of small wars driven by economic motives. Global economies create opportunities, and new technologies provide the means, to fragment authority and spread small wars in the growing cities of the future. Informal, survival-oriented economies and overtly criminal economies emerge in dense urban areas, as they have in sparsely populated rural zones in the past. As the state weakens, these informal economies break away from the control of state agents and seek to manage violence for their own ends.

Economic problems are not automatically a cause of war. However, the exclusion of parts of society from economic participation and benefit can foster a war economy as the state loses the ability to justify economic conditions. In underdeveloped economies, this takes the form of a search for fungible assets – high-value resources that can be converted in a global economy. In developed economies, the choices are greater. Dependence on information-technology infrastructure can be exploited by criminals. The distinction between legitimate multinational corporations and criminals may blur when the motives are purely economic. As motives turn political, we use phrases like "cyber war" and "cyber-terrorism" to describe the potential impact of attacks through information infrastructure. Lifelines for energy, water, and transportation systems could also be attacked for either economic or political motives, or both.

Privatization and economic motives dominate small wars within states and shape the ways in which they intersect with a global economy. The addition of ideological motives changes the international impact of small wars and can lead to fierce and protracted political conflicts. Ideology and religions often fulfil an identity-building function and may be associated with self-confidence and the urge either to expand into other cultural circles or to clearly dissociate and oppose others. Both religion and ideology have been used to mobilize groups in ethnic conflicts and "Warriors of God" in global terror campaigns.

Small wars have significant consequences for international politics. The trends that have been identified are the privatization of violence, erosion of the governmental monopoly on violence, blurred distinction between war and peace, and merging business with violence. These trends serve to merge social space with battle space, making it impossible to distinguish between combatants and noncombatants. Regular forces begin to lose their importance. As all parts of society participate in the use of force and basic human needs are linked to pervasive violence, war becomes total – a way of life.

CONSEQUENCES FOR SECURITY POLICY

The precondition for a stable peace economy is a clear separation of violence from the economy. The denationalization of war and its economic rationale blur the distinction between internal and external security. When information systems or social infrastructure break down, is this the result of planned attacks or simply failure? When a country's allies are subjected to major terrorist attacks and it increases homeland security, is it at war? States or sections of society may fall victim to unconventional or asymmetrical attacks at any time. Multinational responses are not new to international security policy, but they are still novel for internal security. Differences in national legislation and varying standards for privacy, access to information, police investigation, surveillance, and criminal prosecution impede the transnational fight for state security against criminal organizations and ideologically inspired terrorists. In the future, balanced international cooperation of police, intelligence, and secret services will be more important than purely military alliances.

Security can no longer be seen as the preserve of one department. We cannot rely on interior ministries for internal security and on defence ministries for security beyond our borders. Political, economic, and social developments can all generate threats to security, thus requiring a holistic response. This is as true within states as it is at the international level. Today, responsibility for security solutions rests with national and international institutions that act, for the most part, independently from each other. Their activities will have to be integrated and coordinated in new ways. National agencies compete with each other for resources (particularly in funding and recruiting) but depend upon each other in operations. In an environment of scarcity, this suggests that effective preventive security systems require not only unified control in operations but also common planning for design and procurement, training, preparation, and employment of personnel. Greater emphasis must be placed on joint and combined operations of different security bodies that are mutually dependent.

Strategies to prevent domestic and international violence are difficult to formulate and may be impossible to evaluate. Preventive strategies depend, first, on interest in the conflicts of others and, secondly, on the ability of leaders to mobilize interest for domestic support and international legitimacy. Since interventions can be lengthy and costly, it is often easier for developed countries to support a structural approach to conflict prevention than reactive military engagement in crises. This is a long-term approach, however, which may be applied inconsistently, due to domestic political pressures, and also difficult to substantiate because of uncertain outcomes. Global media play an important part in shaping response through the intensity of their coverage. They may determine how the public responds to events and to both state and non-state reactions and interventions. All military actions become public, increasing the importance of other means of response. Military intervention to end severe violations of human rights or to stop genocide has been justified, however, by the International Commission on Intervention and State Sovereignty in their report, *Responsibility to Protect*.

Deterrence strategies can be a useful way of preventing states from offering sanctuary to terrorists and other violent non-state actors. But this approach affects regimes rather than populations. To affect large populations that might harbour terrorists and criminals, it is essential to make structural changes that meet basic human needs and to win "hearts and minds". In turn, this requires international institutions that can make rapid decisions and lead a coherent international community to take effective action. This is a creative political task that has yet to be tackled.

SECURITY POLICY – SHAPING GLOBAL SECURITY

A coherent security policy to address the problems of small wars requires shaping the global community. The most developed states must assume their primary responsibility for civilization and security. Demographic development, environmental change, globalization of the economy, access to information, and sharing of knowledge must become part of a cooperative world order. What must be developed are interdepartmental and intergovernmental instruments that will permit lasting changes to political, economic, and social development policy, the prevention of violence, and the civil management of conflict. Very few "small wars" can be won, but it is possible to contain them while these broad changes are undertaken.

Security risks are inevitably interdependent. The dividing line between war and peace will be increasingly difficult to discern, and preventive security can no longer be achieved at the national level alone, nor by departments working in isolation. Despite our technical achievements, the vulnerability of post-modern industrial states is increasing, particularly with regard to asymmetrical threats. From these changes in the security environment, we can draw conclusions about the consequences for national armed forces.

As part of a comprehensive strategy, the armed forces of civilized nations will have to contribute to the stabilization and maintenance of an economically, socially, and politically dynamic world order. Military planners will have to reconceive the nature of such contributions, which include the ability to maintain a world order that permits equitable development and the ability to intervene in armed conflicts if they present a threat to international security. Conceptually, military planners must be prepared for new actors, new forms of conflict, new tasks, and new technical innovations.

To address these new challenges, we will need armed forces with a high degree of flexibility, professionalism, and capacity to learn. Military leaders must be willing to question existing structures and concepts to permit the armed forces to evolve as learning organizations and to contribute to shaping responsive security policy.

We are on the cusp of global transformations that should be seen as an opportunity to create a future that is more peaceful and worthwhile for all, not just for privileged elites. This requires, however, that whole societies become intellectually involved in defining and pursuing security, not just to fight the symptoms of violence, but to address their deeper causes. In this context, military forces are only one of many instruments to stave off threats. Thus, only where there is a genuine opportunity to improve the political situation can military operations be justified, both to soldiers and to society.

NOTE

1.   This chapter is based on work at the Centre for Analyses and Studies of the *Bundeswehr*.

three

Operation SADBHAVANA
A "Culture of Peace" Process in Kashmir

Leena Parmar

The world is witnessing increasing assertion of collective rights and privileges on the basis of religion, ethnicity, and nationality. Religious fundamentalism, together with ethnic conflicts and terrorism, has appeared in the international arena with remarkable pervasiveness and force. With these changes, traditional ideas about security have become outdated. We have to redefine security not only in terms of military power but also in terms of economic power and the social roles it plays in the nation state. We must ask, security for whom, and how do we achieve it? This chapter is about a novel approach to the protracted conflict in India's Kashmir province. It stems from a visit to Ladakh and Kashmiri border areas where I saw for myself "Operation SADBHAVANA" ("Goodwill") and the extraordinary efforts of the Indian Army's Lieutenant-General Arjun Ray, VSM, General Officer Commanding India's 14th Corps, based in Leh. Operation SADBHAVANA is a long-term strategy for the integration of Jammu-Kashmir into the rest of the country by transforming the life of border villages in Kashmir. It may be relevant to other conflicts where different levels of human security have fuelled ethnic and religious violence over generations.

Kashmiris in India seem indifferent to the rest of the country. When asked about this, Kashmiris may use the phrase: *"hum to mile thae – ap ne alag rakha."* ("We joined you, but you kept us separate.") There is some truth to this. Ending the geographical and political isolation of Kashmir should be one of India's foremost objectives. Transport links and an end to Kashmiri dependency will help to manage the conflict. Economic aid and investment should be geared to allow Kashmir's economy to grow from below with an appropriate development model that is both systematic and sustainable.[1] This is as important for India's relationship with Pakistan as it is for security in Kashmir.

At the heart of the Indo-Pakistani conflict, there are two constraints. The first is the political utility of the war-like tensions between the two countries, and the second is the mutually sustaining mindsets that recognize war as the only real solution. Both India and Pakistan are constantly vulnerable to the urge to fight. Millions of people in both countries are beset by the drudgery of peace. Military preparedness and the news of impending war have the unfortunate capacity to give both the young nation-states an instant sense of purpose. One cannot help recalling a time in the 1970s when India derived a similar sense of purpose by acting as a force for world peace. But it began to lose that sense of identity, even as the failure of the economic development projects of the 1960s became all too apparent. A new national identity began to take shape alongside Cold War models. Hunger, poverty, and illiteracy gradually ceased to inspire the state's planning apparatus. The self-image of military power began to serve a cohesive political role.[2]

Both India and Pakistan have used education and the media to reinforce hostile attitudes. In Pakistan, school textbooks openly teach prejudice towards Hinduism and equate India with Hindus, forgetting India's struggle for secularism. Elite public schools have a better record, but their products either migrate or learn to live on the margins of a fluid, routinely manipulated public space. That journey to the margin of a rapidly shrinking political space is just beginning for the Indian elites whose children have been raised on the staple scientific diet in a corrupt and chaotic political milieu. The simplistic secular textbooks they have studied fail to provide a rational historic context for Partition. This leaves adequate room for the belief that Pakistan is neither a legitimate historical entity nor a functioning nation. Here lies the root of a common perception among Indian elites that India can emulate what Israel has done to a defenceless Palestine. Both India and Pakistan are caught in the cycle of armament that such hostility engenders. Dutch sociologist W. F. Wertheim has criticized the absence of a peace economy in the sole remaining superpower. For India and Pakistan, no less than for Third World states from Chile to the Philippines, escalating tensions and armament offer no hope of peace. A phased disengagement from the arms trade and a new approach to peace might.[3]

My visit to Ladakh and the Kashmir border regions afforded the opportunity to meet villagers and to speak, to schoolchildren and women in particular, about the unique development process envisioned by Operation SADBHAVANA. Building on that experience, I have used content analysis of some leading newspapers and extensive unstructured interviews with more than 150 people from a cross-section of society in the border areas. Interview subjects included men, women, and children drawn from different religious groups. Several focus-group meetings allowed me to meet as many people as possible within a limited time. People were eager to speak, spontaneous, and visibly enthusiastic after years of neglect.

Content analysis is used in social science to study communication – its nature, underlying meanings, dynamic processes, and the people who are engaged in talking, writing, or conveying meaning to one another. Each content analysis employs an explicit, organized plan for assembling the data and classifying or quantifying them to measure the concepts under study, examining their patterns and interrelationships, and interpreting the findings. Sorokin's classic work drew on art, music, and literature, while Lasswell developed schemes for characterizing patients' responses as pro- or anti-self and pro- or anti-other, counting the frequency of occurrence of each. Lasswell also pioneered the application of content analysis to the study of public opinion and propaganda – an effort stimulated by the American government during the Second World War.[4] In the spirit of these inquiries, I have drawn on newspapers and magazines to analyze the reality and assess the success of Operation SADBHAVANA.

CONCEPTS

How do we define peace? For my purposes, a useful definition has to include both the absence of direct violence and the absence of indirect or structural violence. Yet this is a rather negative way to define peace, and several researchers and educators on the subject have attempted to arrive at more positive definitions of the term. One of the more attractive definitions suggests that equality of rights is central: by peace we mean that every member of a society participates equally in the decision-making power that regulates it and in the distribution of the resources that sustain it. UN definitions also strive to describe the positive dimensions of peace, including the presence of justice:

> Peace cannot consist solely in the absence of armed conflict but implies principally a process of progress, justice and mutual respect among the peoples designed to secure the building of an international society in which everyone can find his true place and enjoy his share of the world's intellectual and material resources.[5]

Operation SADBHAVANA is about building a "culture of peace". This is a body of shared values, attitudes, and behaviours based on non-violence and respect for fundamental rights and freedoms, on understanding, tolerance, and solidarity, on the full participation and empowerment of women, and on the free flow and sharing of information. A culture of peace is a vast project linked to economic security and development, political security and democracy, military security and disarmament, cost-benefit analysis and economic conversion, and the development of global solidarity. A culture of peace can flourish only where the functions of war have been replaced by positive alternatives. As General Ray, the author of Operation SADBHAVANA, argues: "A culture of peace should be elaborated within the process of sustainable, endogenous, equitable human development; it cannot be imposed from the outside."

THE HISTORICAL PROBLEM

India and Pakistan were born of Partition – one of the most savage separations of people and territory in the 20th century. Since 1947, they have fought four wars over Kashmir and Bangladesh. India accuses Pakistan of open support for cross-border terrorism. Mutual suspicion rules bilateral relations, and the rest of the world considers the region a potential nuclear flashpoint.

Jammu-Kashmir was one of the 565 princely states of India over which the British ceded control at midnight on 15 August 1947. The ruler of Jammu-Kashmir, Maharaja Hari Singh, was given the option to join either of the dominions – India or Pakistan. He did not exercise this option, but sought a "Standstill Agreement" pending a final accession decision. With Muslims comprising a majority in the Kashmir Valley, one might have expected communal politics to develop, but the people of the region had developed a tradition of tolerance and coexistence. The National Conference led by Mr. Sheikh Abdullah, a popular Kashmiri leader, espoused the nationalism of community interest rather than religion. Pakistani leader M. A. Jinnah failed to win the sympathy of Kashmiri Muslims for his two-nation theory, and it is possible that a plebiscite held soon after Partition might have favoured secular India over Muslim Pakistan.

Pakistani tribesmen entered Kashmir on 22 October 1947, but on 26 October, the Maharaja Hari Singh signed the Instrument of Accession, making Jammu-Kashmir legally part of India. It was not until January 1949 that a cease-fire came into effect, leaving about 54 percent of Jammu-Kashmir under Pakistani control. The region has been a source of conflict ever since, with India and Pakistan going to war over it in 1965, 1971, and 1999.

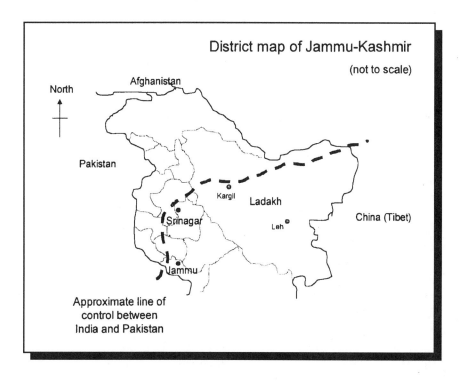

District map of Jammu-Kashmir

Many might argue that the Kashmiri struggle has reached the point of no return. But in reality, the people of the valley are disenchanted, not only with the unending militancy, but also with their manipulation in the power-politics of India and Pakistan. Almost every family has lost a son. Abuse of women has been widespread. The executions of many Kashmiris, including prominent citizens, have left a bitter taste. Power struggles among the militant groups have included kidnapping, looting, raping, killing, and forced marriages of lower-class militants to socially or economically advantaged girls within the communities. All this has generated disenchantment among the average Kashmiri,[6] creating the opportunity for a novel approach to peace-building using the Indian Army.

CONCEPT OF OPERATIONS

General Arjun Ray, VSM, traces the origin of the concept to an incident in 1999. While sitting in his vehicle in a border area, General Ray had waved to some people nearby. They did not wave back – the body language was very clear. Had the Army been alert to such body language earlier, it might have averted the intelligence failure of 1999, when the area of Kargil was infiltrated, without any significant warning, resulting in war with Pakistan. General Ray's conclusion was that human-development policies to make the Indian Army more welcome in the border regions needed to be an intrinsic part of border management.

On his first trip to Turtuk on the line of control, General Ray was greeted by blasts from two improvised explosive devices. As terrified villagers anticipated retribution, Ray unleashed an unexpected dose of development. Turtuk was part of Pakistan-occupied Kashmir until 1971, when India sliced it off from Baltistan. Ethnic affinity with people across the line of control has meant that its Balti-speaking population of about 2,600 have always been under suspicion, and the area has been a flashpoint. At an altitude of 10,000 feet, it played a key role in the Kargil War of 1999, when an intrusion in the area went undetected for months because the locals did not inform the Indian Army – considered an "occupation force". They not only refused logistical support to the Indian Army but are believed to have directed Pakistani shelling. The scene is vastly different today. Development has brought to Turtuk amenities that villages in the hinterland cannot dream of.[7]

Development has come to more than 190 villages along the 284-kilometer line of control from Turtuk to Batalik, Kargil, and Dras, as part of the Army's program in border management. The idea is that winning over the border population by supporting development will help to forestall militancy and infiltration spilling from Pakistani-occupied Kashmir into the Ladakh region, which is part of the border region of Jammu-Kashmir under Indian control.

The Indian Army is an instrument of nation-building, of which peace-building is an intrinsic part. With this objective in mind, the army serves in Ladakh as a facilitator for local governance and administration at the grassroots level. The district administration, non-governmental organizations, and people's representatives have been brought together, and the resources and facilities of the civil administration have been reinforced in these areas. The Army's role of facilitator has been central in involving people in human-development programs in the border regions.

Briefing selected journalists about Operation SADBHAVANA on 10 October 2001, General Ray said, "I planned the SADBHAVANA movement with an aim to stop the infiltration of militants totally." The central objective of the Operation is to prevent the spread of existing militancy from the Srinagar Valley to the Ladakh region. The Operation is intended to sensitize the population of border areas and create an environment that will avoid violent situations while ensuring the all-round development of the region. It has the full support of the Chief Minister of Jammu-Kashmir, Dr. Farookh Abdullah, and the Union Government. Per-capita expenditure for the operation since 1999 is 500 rupees (about US$12), concentrated in the border areas, but this does not imply that the Army has taken over governance of the region. On the contrary, the Army is complementing civil governance. General Ray believes that this sort of development initiative should be undertaken in other tense border regions around the world, with the assistance of funding from the World Bank, the International Monetary Fund, and the Asian Development Bank.[8]

General Ray's operational concept represents a change in the basic definition of the role of the Army. Modern wars, he argues, cannot be won by the power of guns and money. Only winning the hearts of the people will overcome the violence. Armed forces should therefore aim not to win wars but to avoid them altogether. If Indian peacekeeping forces are dispatched to other countries around the world, General Ray asks, why can the Army not be used at home for peaceful nation-building? In speeches in Jammu-Kashmir, people still demand independence but their impact is diminishing. Thousands of educated people from throughout India have volunteered to work for Operation SADBHAVANA in Ladakh, and it is beginning to have an effect.

Operation SADBHAVANA is based on idealism. It relies upon achieving progress through developing mutual confidence within the community. Conventionally in India, the government both plans and executes rural development, but under Operation SADBHAVANA, the local population decide on their needs and make requests of government accordingly. The individual becomes the focus of development. This supports the military logic of General Ray – how can development planning have any focus other than the person? The Army is focussed on protection of people in border villages. The biggest challenge is to prevent infiltration across the border. With China on one side and Pakistan on the other, this is no easy task. Operation SADBHAVANA aims to build local support for a popular, human-based defence, rather than relying on Indian guns and money to control the mass of the population.[9]

SADBHAVANA has begun to change the security situation in Ladakh's border region. Outsiders cannot avoid the locals, who immediately inquire about their names, the purpose of their visits, and so on. They convey this information to the local police or security outpost. Information on horse-traders and vessel-peddlers reaches the police immediately. The confidence of the population is the lifeline of the police and Army operating on the borders. The jawans [soldiers] have been trained for this and so have the appropriate mindset.[10] The local population, which previously harboured militants, now seem to be actively engaged in removing them, resulting in peace for the last 15 months in those areas of Ladakh in which human-resource development programs are being run.[11]

DEVELOPING AND CONDUCTING PEACE-BUILDING OPERATIONS

After the 1999 Kargil War, the Indian Army exerted considerable effort to secure its lines of communication through the Ladakh district along the line of control between India and Pakistan. Social and economic development has been the focus of its efforts. It has built schools, roads, and dispensaries. Thanks to the Army, ten-year-old Rigzen Norbo is now able to play with a computer and speak a little English. Operation SADBHAVANA has meant a new lease on life for many Ladakhi children. Army officers' wives are helping to bring Ladakhi children from remote villages to schools that have been equipped with computers by Bangalore's information-technology industry. Volunteers from Prakruthi, a non-governmental organization based in Bangalore, have come to Ladakh to help teach. K. Lalitha, a volunteer teaching science, said, "I've come here for the first time, and it feels great as it is in the national interest. The general intelligence of the children are [sic] at par with the rest of the country." Encouraged by the positive response, an optimistic General Ray said, "It's a long process. But the locals are realizing that we are doing something for them, and they are with us."[12]

The core concept of Operation SADBHAVANA is that human security is a central element of national security, and it is achieved through human development. Human development, in turn, is necessary for border management. The Army functions as a facilitator but works in close collaboration or symbiosis with district administrators, NGOs, and local representatives. The policy is to reinforce existing resources and facilities of the civil administration and to encourage local involvement in human-development programs. The four main areas in which Operation SADBHAVANA operates are primary education, secondary and tertiary health care, community development, and the empowerment of women.

Primary education has been supported through a network of 16 new "Sadbhavana Schools", but these are schools with a difference. They seek to provide high-quality education based on the National Curriculum. They make extensive use of computers with customized software for teaching English. They provide free meals for schoolchildren and have a non-commercial orientation, with scholarships for children from economically deprived backgrounds. Furthermore, they teach human rights and rights of the child as part of the curriculum, in addition to the more typical religious instruction, and provide special education for mentally and physically challenged children.

The Indian Army supports primary health care in remote villages directly through the actions of unit medical officers. Enhanced primary health and secondary medical care is provided through local clinics and dispensaries supported by the military. Tertiary treatment is provided at the Army's Command Hospital at Chandimandir and PGI Chandigarh. Treatment is free; urgent cases are flown in on military aircraft; and comprehensive follow-up care is available.

Community development has been supported by rural electrification in selected areas. Army engineers have also been involved in village irrigation and anti-drought schemes. Village poultry-farming cooperatives and vocational training for unemployed youths also enhance economic prospects. Resource centres at Leh, Kargil, and Dras support the mentally and physically challenged. An Army-sponsored orphanage has been established at Kargil, and a boys' hostel at Dras. The Army has also sponsored revival of local culture and traditions, supporting polo and archery.

One of the most interesting aspects of Operation SADBHAVANA has been empowerment of women. Human security occurs where there is gender equality, without which human development cannot be sustained. The goals of the operation included improving the status of women in family and community and providing the basic needs to fulfil the traditional roles of daughters and mothers. Beyond this, however, the intent was to provide employment opportunities, health care, and the means for decision-making with respect to reproduction.

The action plan for gender equality includes establishing vocational training centres for nearly 500 girls, with a composite package of education that includes skills in knitting, carpet and shawl weaving, tailoring, or computer literacy. The girls also have the opportunity to upgrade their education through the National Open School Program, supported by new software for senior classes. The centres also provide education in social skills, free lunches, and stipends for students.

Half the funds available for income generation were reserved for women in local village cooperatives in poultry farming. All schoolteachers are also local women. A widow rehabilitation package and working-women's hostels in Leh and Kargil also expand income-generation opportunities for women. The Army has undertaken a massive drive to set up one adult-education centre in each Army unit's area of responsibility. Adult-education centres for non-literate women between 18 and 35 years of age provide 150 hours of assistance to each applicant, including health- and child-care and education in communication skills, folk culture, functional arithmetic, and social education. The aim is to educate at least 3,600 women in each eight-month cycle. A special health program for women and children addresses three vital areas of concern: reproductive health, maternal mortality, and mortality of infants under five years of age.

The results of Operation SADBHAVANA have been impressive. It is operating in 190 villages with a total population of more than a million. It has established 13 Army Goodwill schools, 11 women's empowerment centres, six medical aid complexes, six cooperative poultry farms, a resource centre for challenged children, a women's hostel, a boys' hostel, and an orphanage. In each case, Operation SADBHAVANA has provided the necessary infrastructure, buildings, heating, furniture, equipment, and staff. The Goodwill schools teach 550 students in Leh District and 700 students in Kargil District. The Bal Ashram orphanage houses 47 orphans.

India's Deputy Prime Minister and Home Minister L. K. Advani proclaimed that Turtuk, once a flashpoint, is the one border area in Kashmir where he could walk without any security. Since Operation SADBHAVANA began, 80 men from Turtuk have joined the Army and 32 have joined the police. Among the new soldiers is the son of a retired Pakistani soldier. The man, now 72, retired from the Karakoram Scouts in 1970 and came back home to Tyakshi, which was then part of Pakistani-occupied Kashmir. A year later it was in India. The man's 30-year complaint and only topic of conversation is why Pakistan is not paying him his pension, "Didn't I fight in 1965 against India?" On a recent visit, Minister Advani promised to take up his case with Pakistan. Meanwhile, the Indian Army provides his family with free rations, and his son prepares to defend India.

Can all this goodwill last? Is Sadbhavana attainable? If the project loses momentum, people may see it as a betrayal, and the backlash could be dangerous. "The idea is to make these people self-sufficient so they can stand on their own feet," says Colonel J. S. Pama. "For example, we're building a bus stop near Turtuk. We provide the material, but we have made it clear that they have to provide the labour and maintain it." Charity alone cannot be the engine of growth, although it may be necessary to begin the process because the region has been neglected for so long. Support must be withdrawn gradually for full empowerment – a difficult balance to achieve – and there are already some irritating side effects. A junior officer complains, "Even if we catch someone for theft now, they say, 'We'll complain to General Ray.'"[13]

CONCLUSION

If we want peace to last, we must do everything in our power to expose the crimes committed in the name of nationalism, to propagate universal human rights, democracy, and friendship between peoples. Everyone can do this in some capacity, as parents, grandparents, educators and scholars, journalists and writers, members of neighbourhoods, religious communities, trade unions or women's groups, politicians, or voters. Silence and passivity are not options.[14]

A culture of peace does not deny the conflicts that arise from diversity, but it demands non-violent solutions and promotes the transformation of violent competition into cooperation for shared goals. It is both a vision and a process, a vast project, multidimensional and global, that is linked to the development of positive alternatives to the functions previously served by war and militarism.

A century ago, the philosopher and psychologist William James argued that war would not be abolished until a substitute could be found for the psychological needs it fulfils, such as comradeship, loyalty, and courage. War channels these attributes in action against an enemy. The culture of peace can fulfil such psychological needs equally well through collective struggle against common threats. Non-violence, as described by Mahatma Gandhi and Martin Luther King Jr., is not passive, but active. It requires great courage and strength, harnessed to the struggle against injustice. Moreover, while the culture of war primarily activates young men, the culture of peace provides a focus for everyone – men and women, young and old.[15]

A proud mother, somewhere in the border area near Kargil, remarked, "I have two sons. Both are going to the schools opened by General Ray and are getting the best of education. Now I do not fear for their future. I am sure both my sons will be well-placed citizens of India." I think this is the future of Operation SADBHAVANA.

NOTES

1.   P. Stobdan, "Kashmir: The Key Issues," *Strategic Analysis*, IDSA, vol. XIX no. 1, April 1996.
2.   Krishna Kumar, "Alternatives to National Suicide: Peace as Daily War," *The Times of India*, 13 June 2002.

3. Ibid.
4. International Encyclopedia of Social Science, vol. 3, 4 (NewYork: MacMillan Publisher, 1972).
5. UNESCO, General Conference, XVIII Session, Resolution 11.1 [1974].
6. Stobdan, op.cit.
7. "Now Heart Warfare", *India Today*, 11 June 2001.
8. Vijay Naik, "Sakal", 15 October 2001.
9. Sukrut Khandekar, "Operation Sadbhavana: The Success", *Loksatta,* 15 October 2001.
10. Ibid.
11. Ibid. These include Tyakshi, Bagdang, Partapur, Hunder, Batalik, Chanigund, Darchik, Kargil, Drass, Pandrass, Budkharbu, Nimu, Leh, Karu, Tangste, and Chushul areas of Ladakh district in the Indian-controlled area of Jammu-Kashmir.
12. N. C. Satpathy, Winning People's Hearts in Post-Kargil Ladakh, *The Times of India*, 6 June 2001.
13. Sandipan Deb and Prashant Panjiar, *Outlook*, 20 August 2001.
14. Rohini Hensman, "Peace in South Asia," *Economic and Political Weekly*, vol. XXXVII, no. 19, June 2002: 1805.
15. "UNESCO and a Culture of Peace," UNESCO Publishing, 1997, 18.

four

Non-Mediated Peacekeeping as a Cultural Performance of Masculinity

Deborah Heifetz-Yahav

If the Joint Patrols stop, if they fail, the peace is dead.

Ibrahim (Palestinian Jeep Commander, Tulkarem, 1998)

It is a very important mission. We are here responsible for the fulfilment of the agreement and the application of it into a routine...We are working to get to a situation that will be good for all of us.

Yuval (Israeli DCO Officer, Kalkilieh, 1998)[1]

This chapter summarizes a unique process, which may have wide relevance for protracted conflicts.* It is based upon an ethnographic study conducted from 1997–2000 of two peoples bound to relations of military security cooperation. I have observed Israelis and Palestinians in their barracks, in the field, during their daily meetings, and at conflict-resolution sessions. My argument is that a model of "non-mediated peacekeeping" was created and may be appropriate in other areas to support the transition from war to peace. Differences of military, social, and national cultures may affect the outcome for this sort of peacekeeping.

---

*This chapter is based upon my Ph.D. research. Some parts have been submitted for publication elsewhere.

Working relations between Israelis and Palestinians were a unique socio-political experiment created by the Oslo Agreements of 1993, 1994, and 1995.[2] These set down the cooperative structure that would co-mingle Israeli-Palestinian realities. The Agreements established a paradigm for continuous contact and interaction between Israeli and Palestinian fighters, many of whom shared memories of combat in Lebanon or operations in the territories during the Intifada (1987-1993). Security cooperation functioned in the interstices between fighting and peacekeeping and established what I label "non-mediated peacekeeping." The security apparatus co-operation institutionalized by the Oslo Accords was an attempt to impose calm and build confidence during the "Interim" period before a final peace agreement was to be signed by 4 May 1999. The ethnographic research concentrates on security cooperation as it was performed in the field – within the West Bank and the Gaza Strip – by members of the Israeli-Palestinian Joint Patrols who performed daily in full view of their Palestinian and Israeli audiences.

This chapter makes two points. The first is that the project of the Joint Patrols, and the District Coordination Offices that supervised them, can be understood as an alternative peacekeeping paradigm. The first part of the chapter describes the structure and function of this experiment in non-mediated peacekeeping. It constitutes peacekeeping because trained fighters were assigned the non-belligerent, constabulary task of supporting the transition from war to peace. The second point is that non-mediated peacekeeping between Israelis and Palestinians was a cultural performance that went beyond the instrumental functions of security cooperation. The performance consisted of enactments between security personnel as representatives of their communities. Their work brought together public and private space and drew members of the security cooperation teams into an active negotiation of emotions, trust, and the discovery of similarity. A primary cause for both conflict and solidarity arose from culturally diverse and shared practices of masculinity.

NON-MEDIATED PEACEKEEPING

Starting in May 1994, Palestinian and Israeli military men, armed and side by side, were assigned a constabulary role to keep the peace and protect their respective citizens. In what both sides described as a "bubble," insulated and detached from the surrounding military operations, the Joint Patrols enforced an alliance. They persisted until they were disbanded in October 2000. On 29 September 2000 at 6 a.m., the morning after Ariel Sharon visited the Temple Mount, a Palestinian joint patrolman – a five-year veteran – shot and killed his Israeli counterpart. This event and the dissolution of the Joint Patrols the following month were predicted to be the end of the peace process – a prediction made by both Israeli and Palestinian involved in security cooperation. Indeed, the events marked the beginning of renewed bloodshed that persists today.

The Joint Patrols consisted of pairs of jeeps, one Israeli and one Palestinian, that patrolled the main streets of eight Palestinian cities on the West Bank and two seams along the Gaza strip. Their joint mission was to "ensure free, unimpeded, and secure movement along the roads and in other areas".[3] Israeli citizens – primarily Arab Israeli – and Palestinian residents of the West Bank and the Gaza Strip witnessed the procession every day within the area under Palestinian authority (Area A).[4]

On a typical 24-hour workday, eight men from the military police – four Israeli and four Palestinian – served one of four, eight-hour shifts. They made one run every hour up and down the assigned street at a speed of approximately 35 km/hr. The jeeps were required to stay together at all times whether on patrol or at the Rest Stop, where the men spent up to eight hours sitting, eating, talking, laughing, keeping distance, provoking or threatening each other while taking their break near jeeps parked side by side. Joint Patrols consisted of direct, unmediated communication. The two jeep commanders maintained contact via a joint radio as they tended to various constabulary problems and made humanitarian gestures. These problems ranged from car accidents between Israelis and Palestinians and traffic violations by Israeli citizens to crimes such as drug trafficking or the capture of stolen vehicles. Humanitarian gestures included escorting an injured Palestinian soldier by the Israeli jeep into Israel for admission to an Israeli hospital. (While the reverse also occurred, as when an Israeli soldier was brought by Palestinian ambulance to a Palestinian hospital, this did not involve the Joint Patrols because their mission was not only to keep the roads clear but also to isolate Israeli citizens from contact with the Palestinian police force.)

The suspicion that Israelis would receive unfair or dangerous treatment by armed Palestinian police underlay security cooperation. At the macro level, the Israel Defence Forces (IDF) had unequivocal control over the majority of the West Bank and the Gaza strip. Simultaneously, the Palestinian Authority (PA) operated other security forces within Areas A and B, which created internal struggles within the security apparatus of the PA. The security co-operation infrastructure was entirely separate from other security forces in control of the West Bank, functioning simultaneously but autonomously within the IDF and the Palestinian Security Forces, including intelligence cooperation. In other words, the military security cooperation, structured by the Oslo Accords, was a discrete security instrument that represented a modicum of neutrality and equivalence used to support the transition to peace.

The Joint Patrols were situated within a well-structured security cooperation apparatus. An equal number of Israeli and Palestinian military professionals were assigned to senior positions. The Joint Coordination and Cooperation Committee for Mutual Security Purposes, or Joint Security Committee (JSC), was established as a legal body. Although the Israeli JSC commander sat in Tel Aviv and the Palestinian JSC Commander in Ramallah, each side had between five and seven officers, and all decisions were made by agreement. Meetings were scheduled every two weeks and, when necessary, convened within forty-eight hours. They were hosted alternately by each side, unless otherwise agreed. The JSC provided directives to the two Joint Regional Security Committees (the RSCs) and the ten Joint District Coordination Offices (the DCOs).

The Regional Security Committees (one in Gaza and one in the West Bank) guided DCOs on security policy. Security issues were sent to it by the DCOs, to "ensure proper transfer of information and guidelines to the relevant DCOs and to propose to the JSC security policy guidelines and forward issues to the JSC for determination."[5] Israeli and Palestinian RSCs became legally bound to maintain contact through "regular as well as special meetings...held between the commander of the Israeli military forces and the commander of the Palestinian Police in the West Bank or in the Gaza Strip, as appropriate."[6] The office would be required to operate 24 hours a day "with direct and constant communication links between the two sides."[7]

DCOs were under the command of their respective RSC branch but were directly responsible for the Joint Patrols. The Oslo Agreements created a total of eight DCOs in the West Bank to supervise eight districts. Jenin, Nablus, Tulkarm, Kalkilieh, Ramallah, Bethlehem, Hebron, and Jericho, roughly 2% of the West Bank, were identified as Area A under the Palestinan Authority's complete civil and security control. Two DCO offices, already established in 1994 by Oslo I, were located at the Erez crossing and at the Nuriya Camp for the Khan Yunis district. The DCO consisted of building complexes created after Oslo and constructed either on the boundary between Areas B or C and A, or entirely in Areas B or C. They were military barracks, which in the West Bank were fenced in and divided by flags and fences.[8] Barbed-wire fences surrounded the DCO, and access to the compound was strictly guarded. A team of up to six officers from each side was required to continuously staff each DCO, and DCO commanders were required to review, investigate, and report to their RSC on the overall situation within the DCO's respective district.

Each DCO managed the Joint Patrols within its district. Israeli and Palestinian DCO commanders jointly decided where and when to meet, who would examine a problem between Israeli and Palestinian citizens, or how to manage an incident of mutual concern. As the higher authority, they most frequently dealt with problems related to work or relationships between the Joint Patrolmen in the field or problems between citizens. The DCO was responsible for coordinating the two sides during rock-throwing incidents or more volatile incidents, such as Al Nakba demonstrations,[9] as well as tensions and violence between the men on the Joint Patrols.

DCO commanders organized conflict-resolution sessions when needed, generally once every two months, and jointly mediated them. From violations of the Oslo Agreements to "children's games" of honour, provocations and name-calling, both Israeli and Palestinian commanders jointly mediated conflicts between their soldiers and police. Adapting, accommodating, and listening to one another, dealings among Joint Patrol Jeep commanders, senior Joint Patrol commanders, and DCO officers were mediated by the two DCO commanders, who sat side by side. They discussed problems and managed crises as they occurred. Joint efforts to succeed in the cooperative project motivated all labours, including the selection of the individuals assigned to tasks.

The DCO's staff consisted of commissioned officers. Their sole purpose was to fulfil the Oslo Agreement and maintain diplomatic and peaceful relations between their men, containing tension and resistance in the field. I refer here to conflicts ranging from mundane petty crimes to civilian resistance against military occupation. Responsibility for maintaining professional practice applied to both Israeli and Palestinian. DCO officers were selected for the cooperative task and underwent training in their respective security forces. Over a period of two to three months, Israelis and Palestinian DCO officers studied separately the culture and manners of the opposite side, as well as the logistics of the Oslo Accords and its application to their work.

The Oslo Agreements established a formal change in relations of power. Through numerous seemingly insignificant details that wielded profound symbolic impact, tensions could be assuaged, relations of power negotiated, and working relations built or destroyed. These representational and emotionally significant details were not only improvised, but also written into the text of the Oslo Accords. The Agreements specified which patrol car would lead, and under what conditions. For example, as the jeeps pulled out of their Rest Stop or switched positions during the patrol, they fulfilled Article III, 4.d. in the Agreement, which states that "(o)n roads under Israeli security responsibility, the Israeli vehicle will be the leading vehicle. On roads under Palestinian security responsibility, the Palestinian vehicle will be the leading vehicle."

Palestinian and Israeli patrolmen not only choreographed and synchronized the movement of their jeeps, but also entry into and departure from territorial space, the timing of their work schedules, or even who would talk to or touch whom during the investigation of a car accident. Thus Israelis interrogated Israelis and Palestinians interrogated Palestinians, and this was varied and improvised depending upon where the event occurred. Should an incident transpire in Area A, it was expected that the Palestinian officer would assume the leadership position and in Area B, the lead would be taken by the Israeli officer. Improper protocol could constitute an infraction of the Oslo Accords and become a subject of contention to be discussed at conflict-resolution meetings.

While the jeeps traversed their course, the men on the Joint Patrol managed to engage in the public spectacle. Properly timed and coordinated precision moves and orange flags identified the jeeps as belonging to the Joint Patrols. Joint Patrolmen were brought together despite their backgrounds for the task of security cooperation. Israeli and Palestinian police and soldiers, whether by choice or duty, enacted a relationship to counteract years of humiliation, irreverence, suspicion, cruelty, and pain. At the extreme, the same Palestinian men – Intifada activists, "terrorists or freedom-fighters" who had thrown rocks, constructed Molotov cocktails, or planted bombs – worked the Joint Patrols with the same Israeli men who had interrogated, chased, or imprisoned them during the Intifada from 1987 to 1993. Others, their senior commanders, recalled the Lebanon war in 1982, when each belonged to the opposing side.

The Theatre of War was a fledgling Theatre of the Peace, or perhaps a Theatre of the Absurd. Theatrical metaphors emerged from the patrolmen themselves. Israeli and Palestinian patrolmen complained that their work was an absurd show or "a game of make-believe friendships." Their narratives inspired the insight that their work was experienced simultaneously as a game and as a performance.

While the men saw themselves in a game of teasing and winning, there was another level of meaning at stake. The theatrical metaphor revealed the domain of "make-believe". Narratives of the men revealed a discourse over masking and authenticity among soldiers and military police.[10] Struggles arose that concerned "fakeness" and trustworthiness. Consequently each task – as well as the stage, props, and expressive gestures – possessed meanings that were often mixed and contradictory. The drama over identity bound it to authenticity. Furthermore real soldiering, true "Palestinian-ness" and "Israeliness" could not be disentangled from their identities as real men. In other words, one vital aspect of the drama was the emergence of divergent masculinities that were acted and re-enacted during the daily performance of security cooperation. Consequently, the Joint Patrols were a performance over resources and identity – part ritual, part game, and part make-believe – embedded in an ongoing saga with no real climax, finale, or winner in sight but set in an arena where men as men and as soldiers contended with a political transition.

As a military/security project the Joint Patrols fulfilled a role "betwixt and between",[11] a condition faced as well by members of peacekeeping forces.[12] Peacekeeping research revealed social mechanisms similar to those that transpired on the Joint Patrols. As with the Israeli-Palestinian Joint Patrols, analogous sentiments of ambivalence and ambiguity faced the warriors serving as peacekeepers on the Somalia project, Operation Restore Hope. It was found to be "a confusing mission for American military personnel."[13] As with UN peacekeepers, confusion, boredom, and despair appeared often in the narratives of the Joint Patrolmen, who had the additional and confounding role requirement of making a comprehensive transformation from enemies to partners in peace-building.

Literature about UN peacekeeping raises at least two relevant points for the Joint Patrols. The first concerns adaptability. Shamir and Ben-Ari discuss the future "face" of the military, where modern armies must contend not only with modern information technologies but also with a blurring of distinctions between civilian and military operations.[14] These blurred distinctions characterize the conflicts seen on the Joint Patrols. Palestinian civilians and their quasi-military forces were in a shared struggle for self-determination. Military duty and the political civilian struggle for national self-determination existed as a unified whole, which framed Palestinian professional practice within a political discourse. By contrast, Israeli military and border police created professional distinctions. The practice of professional ethics and discipline bracketed the men and their work as a professional project, not a political exercise. Contrasting political and professional frames revealed an underlying divergence in how Palestinians and Israelis construed the notion of masculinity.

The second point from peacekeeping literature is the tension between constabulary and military ethics. Segal *et al.* express doubts about compatibility "between the parachutists' creed and the constabulary ethic."[15] Shamir and Ben-Ari, on the other hand, consider these changes to reflect two major themes. First, the army is "opening", blurring the traditional borders between military and civilian spheres. This opening demands that the army operate within inter-organizational frameworks involving other forces and non-military organizations.[16] Second, the haziness of professional and political boundaries enables the soldiers' emphasis to shift from fighting and winning wars to deterring conflict, ensuring the fulfilment of agreements, and performing tasks, such as mediating between rival forces, that are normally reserved for constabulary forces. The Joint Patrols are part of this process. Peace campaigns placed military leaders in close contact with civilian populations and civilian bodies. Like the UN peacekeepers, they were engaged in what Alan James identified as the three categories of UN peacekeeping: finger-pointing, face-saving, and fire-watching.[17] All three elements comprised the work of the Joint Patrol/DCO project and further suggest the relevance of conceptualizing the Joint Patrols as a form of peacekeeping, albeit mutated.

Like the UN peacekeepers, Israelis and Palestinians were unable to actively affect the balance of power held by other security forces from which they were isolated. While the hope existed that cooperation would build trust and peace, the men could not escape the contradictions embedded in the political and organizational structures. The primary mission of militaries is combat, and all members must be prepared to fight. The fighter must have ready access to the warrior strategy, which treats "an entire population as potential enemies".[18] Palestinians and Israelis could not be expected to assume the constabulary ethic of "absolute minimal force and impartiality",[19] particularly within the internal and political contradictions of military policy and the prevailing ambivalence regarding how and when the Middle East conflict would be politically resolved. Furthermore, the knowledge that, should the peace process fail, they would revert to their previous roles loomed as a real possibility and intensified the sense of mask-wearing friendliness. Despite these conflicting forces, Israeli and Palestinian fighters transformed the "Other" from an object of fear and distrust into a subject whose behaviour would be familiar and predictable.

NON-MEDIATED PEACEKEEPING AS CULTURAL PERFORMANCES OF MASCULINITY

When the Joint Patrols were created as a way of learning to have confidence in one another, the men were, so to speak, handed a script to build relationships as reliable professionals. Indeed, the assignment of working together, to discover the similarities of one's enemies, could be cynically framed as a process for getting to "know the enemy". Their strategies created proximity and similarity that, whether inadvertently or by design, forged a mutually adaptive process.

The men negotiated their relations through performances and adaptations, developing new moves aimed at reframing each other as professional Israeli and Palestinian men. Positioning the relationship within a gender construct enables a view into what men consider essential in establishing the "Other" as similar. According to Collinson and Hearn, "naming men as men"[20] makes problematic what reproduces men and their masculinity in the daily tasks of security cooperation. Carrigan's theory of "multiple masculinities" describes the cultural, spatial, and temporal diversity of masculinity.[21] The actions of these military men are expressions of men's power and male identity, whether as the patriarchal father/commander or as the brother/comrade in arms. Consequently, soldiers and policemen from the two security forces achieved workable relations of trust through two different domains – the professional and the social – associated with the successful accomplishment and reproduction of their masculinities. I consider below four aspects of the Israeli-Palestinian relationship: the nature of the working man, divergent concepts of professionalism, the problem of Palestinian professionalism and Israeli control, and solidarity between "men of war".

THE PROBLEM OF THE WORKING MAN

Iyad (Palestinian DCO Officer, NW)

Q: What have you learned from doing this work?

A: Israelis feel, sleep and eat – they are human like we are and that is the way it should be. I believe in this work, that it can make everything better for the two peoples. And we will work hard.

Yuval (Israeli DCO Officer, NW)

Q: What surprised you the most in your experience with the Palestinians?

A: Again, to see that they are people like you and you think like them – that they think and talk like me and that I work with a Palestinian officer and could imagine wanting to draft him as an officer in the Israeli Defense Forces.

Contact through working relations not only changed the attitudes of Palestinian and Israeli security personnel but also exposed themes of a perceived similarity. Two different strategies of bracketing the "Other" emerged. Their approaches may be seen in part as a dualism of body and mind. In the Palestinian example, the officer framed Israeli humanity in a shared physical experience – to "feel, sleep and eat", since Israelis, too, are "human." According to his narrative, Israeli humanity was discovered through contact and a working relationship. Similarity began in the physical experience and built into a political conceptualization of collective well-being. Although both men were in search of trustworthiness, I argue that they represented two divergent conceptualizations of masculinity. Palestinian masculinity was understood as a totality inseparable from politics and patriarchy. Israeli masculinity was understood as separable units of meaning bound to a rationality of professional ethics and skill.

In the quote above, the Israeli affirmed the standards of Palestinian officers as professional army men who exhibited a level of competence. He saw his Palestinian counterparts as men he would want "to draft to the IDF" as part of his trusted, professional team. He did not frame Palestinians as men who shared similar embodied experiences as men, but as professional military men whose skill and competence established bonds of solidarity and similarity.

Noam (Israeli JP Jeep Commander, Nezarim Junction, Gaza)

We are an army with values – a police with values – we work in an organized manner – *"mesudar, memusad"*. We take this business very seriously. With them, it's not. Look, I blame them, and I don't blame them. With them, the

business works from day to day. You see that it is not well structured or organized. They have neither the conditions nor the means. They also don't
have ethics or values. They have no problem to lie to you in your face.

Noam's accusation that his counterparts do not "take this business very seriously" reflected a critical breaking-point that
undermined the very similarity being conceptualized. Military
honour and military ethics required clear guidelines of practice.
It was not an improvised game that "works from day to day." According to Noam, his counterparts did not share the same
interactional rules, the very process of morality associated with
ideals of military masculinity – the "honour code", which requires
"complete truthfulness in every regard."[22] The question is whether
the acts required for manhood were conceived to be the same by
both Palestinians and Israelis.

The men working on the JP and in the DCO were not trying to
control the meaning of masculinity. Rather, they were negotiating
the coexistence of each other's manhoods. Being good at being a
man may reside not only in professional skill but also along the fine
line between control and loss of control involved in maintaining
proper poise.[23] For the Palestinian ideal, "real men" not only hold
their poise but also display the skill to protect another's "Face".[24]

Palestinian demands focussed primarily on changes in Israeli
behaviour with regard to "Face" and honour, while Israelis identified
professional standards and ethics as their primary concerns. For example, whether the patrols met at the DCO or at the Rest Stop, there
were crucial elements to the initial encounter, which affected the functioning of the JP. Only once the men had engaged in rites of
acknowledgement could the Joint Patrol begin. Each man would shake
hands and exchange words of greeting with the other. First the officers shook hands. Then the Palestinian officer shook the hands of the
Israeli policemen, while simultaneously, the Israeli officer shook the
hands of the Palestinian policemen. If at any point, a policeman refused to shake hands with someone from the other team, particularly
the officer, it would be interpreted as a grave insult. In many such
circumstances, the Joint Patrol was cancelled on the spot. Thus, proper
greetings and appropriate touching constituted critical moments of
contact. Face and handshakes became two of many learned cultural
imperatives. Israelis, in order to successfully engage Palestinians in
working relations, needed to acquire a new set of dispositions and
practices. The same can be said of the Palestinian, but the domains
were different.

Palestinians and Israelis were searching for trust in two different arenas – the professional and the social/political. In an attempt to prove trustworthiness, Israelis tested Palestinian professional practice. By contrast, Palestinians evaluated Israeli credibility through their reproduction of social structure and a perceived shift in relations of power. Both sets of narratives were thus concerned with performances that constructed, devalued, or upheld culturally bound notions about masculinity. Disciplined values were both conceptualized and acted out, relating masculinity to relations of power and expressions that could shift the balance of military or political asymmetry. Yet their conceptualizations coalesced at the site of trust.

Both Israelis and Palestinians claimed to be in search of trust, and their shared concerns bound trustworthiness to manliness. Narratives identified each side's expectation of the other to meet demands of professional practice. Israeli willingness to shift control over to Palestinians, to support Palestinian capacity, depended in part on perceptions of the Palestinian trustworthiness. Palestinians did not have to "be" similar but had to behave similarly as professionals. And while the Israelis tested whether Palestinian military men performed reliably and consistently, Palestinians saw themselves as fully committed to the task, having compromised by facing their people as collaborators in every negative sense of the term. For their part, Palestinians' concern over professionalism was not bound to Israeli trustworthiness. They framed Israeli practice as acts that would shift relations between occupied and occupier. For Palestinians, actions were more important in terms of their political meaning than of military protocol.

DIVERGENT PROFESSIONALISMS

The concern Israeli officers expressed over military ethics and consistency in professional practice contrasted with the Palestinian officers' attention to physical interaction, power, and citizenship. Palestinians saw Israelis engaged in a choreography of equivalence that reinforced their need for Face. When Khalil, the Palestinian commander of the RSC, states that Palestinian soldiers are being trained as professionals, what did he have in mind?

> Our men are trained to be quiet and calm and to know their job. We respect and admire the Israeli way. The respect should not be for the person, but the orders. Not for the person who gives the order. From our experience, the relation between soldiers and officers is good ... There are some differences in leadership

style, but in the military law, to hit a soldier is not acceptable. In our culture, it may happen. We are growing in the direction of becoming professional. In every State there must be a professional army and police that are well organized, that will be necessary for our government, state and for the peace in the future.

The senior Palestinian Commander draws a direct parallel between professionalism and physical expression. To be quiet and calm – to acquire the poise – requires professional training. These are qualities conceptualized as a requisite value of military men who "know their job." His narrative supports the earlier observation of the sensuality of manliness through poise. Thus, the senior Palestinian military commander identified the need to develop professional Palestinian military behaviour and acknowledged that Israeli standards can serve as a model.

Like the Palestinians, Israelis were also concerned about men suited for the task; however, they talked about professionalism in thought, ethics, and practice. A person's expressive repertoire was not subjected to training.

> Q: What are the important ingredients that make the patrols work?
> Dan (Israeli RSC Commander): Personalities. We remove people who are impulsive, who take every move as personal honour or lack flexibility. Their politics is less important.
> Faruq (Palestinian DCO Commander, C): No, it depends upon their politics. Everything is political.
> Dan: Perhaps these qualities are consistent with their political bent, but for us, our work is very sensitive, and if they see someone not fitting, we send them out – it is true for both sides.

The Israeli framed his professionalism through the ability to meet instrumental tasks. According to Dan and other DCO commanders, men at the DCO were brought into the work with the specific personality traits suitable for the cooperative task at the DCO. It was not expected that the training would make the man, but that the selection would find the men who would not "take every move as personal honour or lack flexibility". Since the "work is very sensitive", human resources staff had selected individuals able to fulfil the professional mission at the DCO. While the Palestinian commanders also said that their men were selected, I found that their primary concern was political association. As Faruq indicated, "it depends upon their politics. Everything is political." Hence, politics was bound to professionalism – an inseparable totality uniting masculinity, politics, and emotion.

Palestinian Professionalism and Israeli Control

The ability of Palestinians to exhibit their value as effective military men was, by definition, limited. Israelis measured professionalism through acts in which Palestinians obediently abided by Israeli protocol as outlined in the Oslo Agreements. This attitude created professional asymmetry and handicapped Palestinian efforts in the field. But if overall control rested with Israelis, control of the personal interactions within the joint patrols was dominated by the Palestinians, who sought to make Israeli behaviour conform to their ideas of Face and appropriate deportment. This, in turn, was an effort to adjust the power structure, rather than simply function as professional collaborators with the Israeli occupation.

> Hani (Palestinian DCO Officer, NW): We get along well with the Israelis at the DCO. But the work of the JP in the agreement should not be limited only to Area A. We must work everywhere, throughout the West Bank. We must work everywhere where problems exist between the Israelis and Palestinians.
>
> Q: What is your authority?
> A: The DCO has the authority to change every six months. The Agreement is not the Koran – it is not the *Tanach* [Old Testament]. We learn the lessons of the daily work, and this should give us flexibility.
> Q: Do the Israelis understand?
> A: No, they don't understand anything. The problem is in the Israeli side – they don't know what to do.

Hani acknowledged that he and his comrades "get along well with Israelis" but noted that the continuance of asymmetric access undermined Palestinian expertise. According to Hani, equalizing relations of power by granting equal police sovereignty throughout the West Bank would enable Palestinians to create the type of individuals that Israelis sought. The Oslo Agreement was "not the Koran...[or] the *Tanach*." Yet Israelis resisted applying the "lessons of the daily work" that would have given the Palestinian security forces "flexibility." The dismay over improvization, described above by Israelis as unprofessional, was met by Hani's demand for precisely that, i.e. greater flexibility and adaptability. In lieu of improvizations to adjust relations of power, IDF practices reproduced the asymmetry through checkpoints and other missions of general security. Israelis abided by the book. In other words, the lack of control and access over their own people revealed, according to Hani, that the Israelis "don't understand anything...[that] they don't know what to do." This was not a criticism of individual Israelis from the DCO and JP, but of the collective practices of the IDF beyond the bounds of military security cooperation. While the Palestinians were fulfilling their professional work as best they could, without Israeli adaptation of a shift in control, the Israelis would neither achieve security nor successfully test Palestinian professionalism.

The plea to be trusted was heard in some Palestinian narratives as a strategic request for more power in the field. Simply communicating factually accurate details could not be disassociated from interpretation – both Israelis and Palestinians complained. The ambiguity about the peace process and the interim phase of security cooperation not only made the relations unclear but made the interpretation of the relations hazy and thus the feelings that accompanied the process difficult to decipher. Despite who was in control and who was not, no one knew who was honest and who was not, and both sides were joined in the same limbo state. What constituted professional behaviour diverged for the two sides. While the Palestinians asked for trust and the flexibility to solve problems, the Israeli soldiers measured Palestinian professionalism by adherence to military ethics and values. These ethics were manifested not only in how Palestinians spoke, in whether "Palestinians have no problem to lie to you in your face", but also in the embodied practices displayed as military discipline, reliability, and consistency. When Israelis referred to professional values and performance among their Palestinian counterparts, they referred to accuracy of making reports, the nature of Palestinian leadership style, the lack of strict weapons-handling procedures, and professional discipline during incidents of violent unrest when close cooperation was critical.

In contrast to the Palestinian narratives, which called for trust and increased symmetry, the Israeli narratives recalled numerous incidents when Palestinians failed to demonstrate their trustworthiness and uphold a professional military ethic. Some Israeli officers framed the dangerous "Other" from the actions of specific individuals. Counteracting the Israelis' search for the military man as a professional, the Palestinians reproduced the native model of Palestinian patriarchy, inseparable from their national struggle. Israeli actions were watched and evaluated on the basis of a discourse of power. Israelis talked about adapting to Palestinian style or feeling Palestinian pain or even injustice. Palestinians talked about how Israelis must accommodate and change to fit their expectations of behaviour. Simultaneously, Israeli professionalism left emotions out of their framing process, while Palestinian native patriarchy recognized emotion as the "glue".[25]

The logic of emotions recognized that the willingness of Palestinians to engage in a relationship depended on the professional willingness of Israelis to adapt. Israeli actors were torn by mask-wearing contradictions, yet their professional ethic kept them in the game. From the Palestinian perspective, voluntary acceptance of a working relationship was itself representative of a great emotional compromise: accepting a Palestinian state within 1967 borders and relinquishing the struggle for pre-1947 Palestine.[26] Therefore, the onus to shift the power relations was placed squarely upon the Israelis.

Although Palestinian narratives varied, a pattern did emerge. Israeli behaviour was framed as "occupation behaviour".[27] They were therefore expected to accommodate and change into tangibly different behaviour; whether by handshakes, "warm" expressions, or the sharing of professional information, Palestinian officers argued that the performance of peace would create the feeling of peace. As one Palestinian officer described it, Israelis must learn to behave according to Arab standards, to abide by Palestinian practices of physical interaction. Through their Israeli counterparts, Palestinian officers indirectly "instructed" Israeli soldiers "not to do that, and that, and that." The content of these instructions focussed both on social conduct as well as on military practice.

> Q: Does the Israeli know how to work with you?
> Khalil (Palestinian RSC Commander): If the Israeli knows how to work with us, this is important. It depends on the officers, both Israeli and Palestinian. At most of our DCOs, the relations work well. We always try to keep good relations with the Israeli officers. [Touches his heart] If the officer who works with the Palestinians makes a promise, he must fulfil it in order to develop trust between us. The Israeli must not act [rising, he puffs out his chest] arrogant. That will make our job easier. We have many problems and the Israeli officers often check out and see [he is referring to checkpoints, searches, and limits on entry permits] to solve these problems. But the situation [the occupation] makes our job difficult and our feelings bad. For example, a policeman wanted to go to Gaza tomorrow. When I will ask, it will take two weeks. The officer says that it is not his responsibility, but there is not anyone who will agree to the permit. So we wait a long time to manage any problem.

Khalil identifies the direct relationship between the Israelis' expressive repertoire (Israelis must not act arrogantly) and the Palestinians' ability to perform basic tasks. Israelis were asked to learn how not to make "feelings bad" in order to accomplish the security-related objectives of conflict-resolution sessions. These sessions both served as a pressure valve to release tensions that arose in the field and facilitated a process of mutual influence.

Solidarity Between Men of War

The material conditions and instrumental practice of security cooperation created a working level of solidarity. Shared living conditions and the various problems that arose from the work served as mechanisms to build a working level of trust. They helped create the emergent situational culture taken into the body, which enabled the work to function, or even to be described as "good."

> Q: Think how you would feel if you were in their place?
> Mati (Israeli Joint Patrolman, Kalkilieh): If I was in their place? In principle they are just like me. But I don't know what it's like to be in their situation. I don't live among them. I know that they earn just like we earn at the DCO, maybe even more. But if I lived in Kalkilieh and couldn't get out of Kalkilieh - that's right [he says quietly] their lives are not easy.

Shared experiences appeared as another source of solidarity. While the Israeli policeman noted that Palestinians "in principle" are like himself, he either could not or would not imagine himself living the life of a Palestinian. His main argument emerged from the fact that he did not "live among them, where they live." In this way, the capacity to embody the "Other" was limited to the inherent barriers of daily life. This point of separation leads to the second aspect of shared living conditions, for although Israeli and Palestinian civilians did not share embodied memories of daily life, military men did. Precisely because they shared the same suffering, uncertainty, and discomfort, at least from the Israeli perspective, life as army men was a unifying factor in their relationship.

> Dan (Israeli RSC Commander): I fought in Lebanon and my Palestinian counterpart also fought in Lebanon, and we would sit and talk about Lebanon together, about the cherries, grapes, girls, trees, and hills. We would remember the wars together. There is a shared language of suffering and humour and they, like me, had also been young men at the time. Sometimes army people have more in common than with civilians - their low salaries and other shared problems.
>
> We tried, from the very beginning, to live and work equally under the same conditions. We had the same mud, the same disgusting chemical toilets - at the beginning it was mutually bad and every improvement we received equally. If we got toilets, so did they. Our flags were equally high to the centimeter. The Palestinian commander could not say that one receives more.

If there were problems, they were solved by both people. Now the real negotiations, the real problem-solving, occur as we walk to meetings, while sitting over coffee. We never meet in the Joint Operations Room created as the
formal context for the mutual negotiations.

But the impact and possibility for these informal negotiations and conflict-
resolution meetings emerge only because of the book – it is the *"Aba Hagadol"*
– the Big Daddy – and within the formal structure it works. It is the living
together, the small day-to-day issues like water, food, clothing, and heating.
In Kalkilieh we were both freezing at night. And it is during these times that
relationships develop. We need the formal context, but it is the day-to-day
informal relations of living together that make this process work.

I remember one night with Faruq. We were freezing cold and on duty while
there were serious problems in the area – it was March 1997 – and we told
jokes all night. Now Arab jokes have their own humour. They are different,
and you must learn how to laugh at them.

Dan identified the equivalence earned from their shared experiences and memories. Recollections from Lebanon – eating
cherries and grapes, looking at girls, trees, and hills – were brought
into the present through the shared suffering of freezing nights,
foul smells, and struggles with instrumental tasks. The endurance
of physical hardships during security cooperation was a military
project that both Palestinians and Israelis overcame successfully.
Conditions of deprivation challenged and were met by both sides.
The cold and putrid toilets not only served as mechanisms to equal-
ize suffering and discomfort among military men but also created
the possibility of an agenda for improvised practice layered with
shared memories and emotions.

Dan: We would ask ourselves and the others when the situation was so bad,
why continue? But we had the command to continue, and we did. It is hard
for an organization to protect motivation, but the commanders acted – all
the DCOs throughout all of the most difficult tests until today has never ceased
to function twenty-four hours a day. There was never a breakdown at the
DCO level. Even during the bombing of Dizengoff, we sat down together and
watched the horrible news on the TV.

The professional interface between feeling the other's pain, protecting motivation, and performing orders was negotiated during
direct physical contact. At the DCO the space was created for mutual
empathy and suffering and as a result, both teams "sat down together
and watched the horrible news on TV." Indeed, Israelis talked about

how the Palestinian people were suffering and the fact that all they wanted was a life. But while the argument "for a life" was shared by both Israeli and Palestinian commanders, the Palestinian narratives held a hidden superiority or legitimacy of Palestinian manhood.

Faruq (Palestinian DCO Commander, C): Look, I fought Israelis in Beirut, but I never hated Israelis. I don't hate any religion or any people.

Q: Did you know Israelis when you were in Algeria?

A: No – of course not. If I had said the word Israeli while in Algeria, they would have killed me. We fought against Israelis in Lebanon in all the battles, in battle of Beirut. I know the Israelis – I was in close range with Israelis when I fought them in Lebanon. Israelis love life more than we do. They are good in their tanks but not when fighting persons. The Israelis are afraid to die, but when you think military, it is not good to feel that way. We knew the Israelis through our Intelligence and we fought at close range. With technology, the Israelis were better [in Lebanon] but with Kalishnikovs, we were better. They love life, but we are willing to die and fight for a life. Now we make peace. Yes, this is good, it is very good – when people who were once enemies are now working as friends.

In this narrative, Faruq described memories of fighting Israelis that identified multiple layers of professional meaning. Faruq conjured not feelings of hatred but an appreciation for the Israelis' love of life. Thus, he not only established the Palestinian's superior frame of suffering – reproduced by their willingness to fight and die "for a life" – but also claimed the Palestinian's superiority as men of valour. Indeed, the ability to sacrifice one's life for the community epitomizes the soldier's creed. Self-sacrifice and bravery are evident in the Arabic term for manly valour associated with *mruwwa*. As Barrett describes in his study of the US Navy,[28] Israelis model mastery over complex, highly technical machinery. Hacker and Cockburn have noted that this is the established domain of men.[29] While the Palestinian DCO commander recalled his feelings towards Israelis during the fighting in Lebanon and the "close range" in which they fought one another, he noted that Israelis have a professional problem. Israeli passion for life was dubious for the professional soldier, for "it is not good to feel that way." Despite Israelis' technical ability with complex instrumentation, Palestinians perceived their own manhood as superior because they sacrificed willingly.

Itzik (Israeli Joint Patrolman, Kalkilieh): What are they doing by delaying us from withdrawing? The Palestinians are truly suffering from it. And it also is expressed here in the field. What could it possibly be: a children's game? We agreed on a peace process, so we should go on with the peace process to the end. And not delay or postpone it. Truly. All the delays create problems in the field.

They request a normal life. They want to do what they want with their lives. Everything that comes to mind, everything that happens in every other place, they also want here.

Deprecating himself and the country he represents as "a children's game", the Israeli Joint Patrolman identifies with the Palestinian request "for a life". The negotiation of multiple masculinities was thus couched in a discourse of solidarity and a struggle over assessing whose masculinity was actually more fully realized. Mastery over machinery or willingness to sacrifice oneself positioned multiple masculinities at odds. Despite the Israeli search for the Palestinian's professional ethics and consistency of performance, Israelis were effectively forced at the micro level of interaction to adapt, not only by relinquishing military power and control, but also by changing their masculine prototype. Changing their expressive repertoire, they reproduced Palestinian sovereignty as "native" men dictating "native" practices. Furthermore, Israelis consistently recognized the Palestinians' struggle as legitimate. A common thread was discovered through working relations, but it was one that weakened the Israeli military man. Mutual agreement recognized the need for professional military practice – although differences existed in what constituted such practice.

CONCLUSIONS

I have argued that the military security cooperation project between Israelis and Palestinians was a constabulary mission performed by soldiers to support the transition from war to peace. I call this social-political experiment a military operation of "non-mediated peacekeeping". Israeli and Palestinian commanding officers faced and resolved problems together. From conflict-resolution sessions to the joint supervision of missions, military security cooperation created a sterile bubble detached from other security forces controlling the West Bank and the Gaza Strip.

At the macro level, the IDF clearly maintained dominance over the majority of the West Bank and portions of the Gaza Strip. Yet, at the micro level, daily contact revealed a different set of power relations that interfaced social, military, and national cultures and *made Palestinian cooperation a negotiated resource*. Through an analysis of multiple masculinities, a vital aspect to daily relations as both adaptive process and power struggle came into view. Israeli military men in search of Palestinian professionalism collided with Palestinian patriarchal nationalism. Both parties in search of trust and similarity were able to find common ground through a professional and embodied discourse. Yet the process revealed an unexpected vulnerability that forced the Israelis to modify and reproduce what constituted "native" masculinity as defined by their Palestinian counterparts. As with UN peacekeepers, the blurred military/civilian (i.e., military/political) divide made precarious an already volatile work task. Despite the internal contradictions and tensions, I have argued that the military cooperation project succeeded, precisely because the men shared goals and allegiance as military men assigned to build peace. The resulting political failure was not contingent upon Joint Patrols or the DCO. On the contrary, political failure was partly the result of misreading how adaptive change and trust could be built. Thus, "non-mediated peacekeeping" as a mechanism to support the transition from war to peace orchestrated by the belligerent parties not only served to reduce violence and build trust, but also to provide a site for witnessing and evaluating needed political/military steps that would enhance the project of peacemaking.

NOTES

1. Names have been changed to protect anonymity and locations abbreviated to NW (Northwest) and C (Central) when necessary to enhance anonymity.
2. (DOP) Declaration of Principles on Interim Self-Government Arrangements, signed in Washington, D.C., 13 September 1993; (Oslo I) Agreement on the Gaza Strip and the Jericho Area, signed in Cairo, 4 May 1994; (Oslo II) Israeli-Palestinian Interim Agreement on the West Bank and the Gaza Strip, signed in Washington, D.C., 28 September 1995.
3. Oslo II, 34.
4. The Oslo Agreements identified land areas in the West Bank and the Gaza strip according to degrees of sovereignty: Area A, which was under civil and security control by the Palestinian Authority; Area B, which was under Palestinian civil authority, but Israel maintained control over security; Area C, which was under Israeli civil and security authority.
5. Ibid., 35–36.
6. Ibid., 36.
7. Ibid.
8. I have not visited the DCO in the Gaza Strip, but was told by a former Israeli DCO commander that no fences separated Palestinian and Israeli sides at the two DCOs located in the Gaza Strip. This was not the case in the West Bank.
9. The Al Nakba is Arabic for "the Catastrophe." It refers to the creation of the State of Israel in May 1948 and corresponds with Israel's Independence Day.

10. Eyal Ben-Ari, "Masks and Soldiering: The Israeli Army and the Palestinian Uprising," *Cultural Anthropology*, vol. 4 (1989): 372–389. See Deborah Heifetz-Yahav, "Non-Mediated Peacekeeping – The Case of Israeli-Palestinian Security Cooperation," in [untitled], Erwin Schmidt and Tom Mockaitis, eds. (London: Frank Cass, forthcoming) for a more thorough discussion of authenticity, mask-wearing, and the negotiation of emotion.

11. Turner, Victor, "Variations on a Theme of Liminality," in *Secular Ritual*, Sally Falk Moore and Barbara Meyerhoff, eds. (Amsterdam, The Netherlands: Van Gorcum, 1977), 37.

12. Charles Moskos, *Peace Soldiers: The Sociology of the United Nations Military Force* (Chicago: University of Chicago Press, 1976).

13. Laura Miller and Charles Moskos, "Humanitarians or Warriors?: Race,Gender, and Combat Status in Operation Restore Hope," *Armed Forces & Society*, vol. 21, no. 4 (1995): 614–637 (615).

14. Boas Shamir and Eyal Ben-Ari, "Leadership in an Open Army? Civilian Connections, Inter-Organizational Frameworks and Changes in Military Leadership," unpublished paper for the symposium on Leadership Challenges of the Twenty-First Century Army (Hebrew University: Wheaton, IL, 1996).

15. David Segal, Jesse Harris, Joseph Rothberg, and David Marlowe, "Paratroopers as Peacekeepers," *Armed Forces & Society*, vol. 10, vol. 4 (1984): 487–506 (506).

16. Shamir and Ben-Ari, "Leadership in an Open Army?"

17. Alan James, "Politics in the UN System: The Issue of Peace and Security," unpublished paper presented to International Studies Association, Washington, D.C. (1985).

18. Miller and Moskos, "Humanitarians or Warriors?, 618.

19. David Segal, Theodore Furukawa, and Jerry Lindh, "Light Infantry as Peacekeepers in the Sinai," *Armed Forces & Society*, vol. 16, no. 3 (1990): 385–403 (387).

20. David Collinson and Jeff Hearn, "Naming Men as Men: Implications for Work, Organization and Management," *Gender, Work and Organization*, vol. 1, no. 1 (1994): 2–22.

21. Tim Carrigan, Bob Connell, and John Lee, "Towards a New Sociology of Masculinity," *Theory and Society*, vol. 14, no. 5 (1985): 551–603.

22. David Mrozek, "The Habit of Victory: The American Military and the Cult of Manliness" in *Manliness and Morality*, J.A Mangan and J. Walvin, eds. (Manchester: Manchester University Press, 1987), 231.

23. David Collinson, *Managing the Shopfloor: Subjectivity, Masculinity and Workplace Culture* (Berlin: Walter de Gruyter, 1992); Cynthia Cockburn, *Machinery of Dominance* (Boston: Northeastern University, 1985); David Morgan, *Discovering Men* (Routledge: London and New York, 1992); Eduardo Archetti, *Masculinities: Football, Polo and the Tango in Argentina* (Oxford: Berg, 1999).

24. Ali Hussein Qleibo, *Before the Mountains Disappear: An Ethnographic Chronicle of the Modern Palestinians* (Kornesh El Nil, Egypt: Al-Ahram Press, 1992), 9.

25. Randall Collins, "On the Micro-Foundations of Macro-Sociology," *American Journal of Sociology* 86 (1981): 984–1014.

26. Hani, Palestinian DCO, NW; Nadim, Palestinian DCO, NW; Faruq, Palestinian DCO, C.

27. Hani, Palestinian DCO, NW.

28. Frank Barrett, "The Organizational Construction of Hegemonic Masculinity: The Case of the US Navy," *Gender, Work and Organization*, 3, 3 (1996): 129–142.

29. Sally Hacker, *Power, Pleasure, and Technology* (New York: Routledge, 1989); Cockburn, *Machinery of Dominance*.

five

To Serve and Protect
The Changing Dynamic of Military and Policing Functions in Canadian Security Policy

Tami Amanda Jacoby[1]

This chapter explores the interface of military and policing roles in Canada's security policy. The main argument is that functions typically associated with national security have been merged with those typically associated with criminal investigations and law enforcement. The purpose of the analysis is to determine the constraints and opportunities implied by this new relationship between military and police for security, democracy, and the future of the military profession in Canada. Understanding these trends requires an integrated approach, drawing concepts, debates, and policy implications from a range of disciplines that includes political science, international relations theory, criminology, and peace studies. Research was conducted through a series of interviews with government officials in Ottawa, augmented by secondary literature, archival, and Internet sources.

The first section of the chapter provides a theoretical foundation for the study, probing conventional definitions of military and policing functions and determining their contemporary relevance. The second section discusses new roles performed by police, intelligence, and the military in the international arena as a result of new forms of conflict and insecurity. The third section evaluates military and policing functions in two major initiatives in Canadian foreign policy: the new human-security agenda and post-9/11 counter-terrorism policy. The chapter closes with remarks about the compatibility of Canadian security policy with liberal democracy.

THE MILITARY

The traditional (realist) definition of the military that evolved during the period of the Cold War viewed the military-industrial complex as the primary security-policy instrument of the state. The military's purpose was to defend against foreign attack, conduct operations overseas, and preserve the state's national security. National security has been defined as the territorial integrity of the state and the security of its boundaries and government. With the establishment of the modern state system since the Peace of Westphalia in 1648, the principles of sovereignty and non-intervention guide states to refrain from interfering in the domestic affairs of other states as a means of upholding international peace and stability. When states do resort to coercive diplomacy to negotiate and achieve their international objectives, the military is the immediate source of capabilities to impose their national interest. This approach follows Clausewitz's well-known dictum that war is a continuation of policy by other means.[2]

Mainstream perspectives hold that military capabilities provide the most important short-term source of national power, measured by the size, composition, preparedness, and effectiveness of a state's armed forces, including army, navy, and air force. Throughout the Cold War era, states invested resources, research, and technological development in their armed forces, adding to their capabilities both qualitatively and quantitatively.

Critics have argued that inherent in this approach is an inclination by states to increase their military capabilities to offset the expected growth of the capabilities of their adversaries. The international arena is viewed as an anarchical system wherein states are motivated by rational pursuit of self-interests. The need for security in a system without global governance leads to an infinite accumulation of weapons, "the chain reaction arms race cycle".[3]

As an extension of conventional military doctrine, functions associated with UN peacekeeping missions overseas since 1948 have emphasized the role of states and militaries as third-party arbiters in inter-state war. Since 1948, the functions of peacekeepers have often been limited to physical positioning between hostile parties, mediating, bringing groups to the negotiating table, and helping to monitor a negotiated settlement. Interposition characterized peacekeeping operations in Lebanon, the Golan Heights, Cyprus, India-Pakistan, and Iraq-Kuwait.

Peacekeeping forces have also been faced with conflicts that are waged in different ways and over issues that are not territorial or military. Intrastate conflicts have been the predominant mode of violence since the Second World War.[4] The correlates of intrastate conflict include poverty, discrimination and other violations of human rights, ethnic tensions, religious prejudices, historical enmities, movement of peoples, changing borders, and competition for diminishing natural resources. The catalogue of possible causes poses "complex security challenges both for individual states and for regional and global security alliances".[5] Peacekeepers face a dangerous and uncertain environment today as they embark upon international missions. The dilemmas accompanying these conflicts have resulted in reforms in organization of the United Nations and in revised understandings about the role of armed force in international conflict situations.

Homeland defence has also undergone a transformation. Military analysts have noted the reduced probability of physical invasion or air attack against states by a military aggressor, with the exception of September 11. The prominent security threat on the Western agenda today is terrorism. Terrorists function through transnational networks, using unconventional weapons (such as chemical and biological agents) and unconventional tactics (hijacking, arson, bombing, and ambush, for example). While lacking the resources of armies, terrorist organizations have been able to mount attacks against urban centres. Writing before the September 11 attacks, Jonathan White argued that "terrorism is too complex and too insignificant to be controlled by nation-states".[6]

In addition to terrorism, new threats on the international agenda are related to humanitarian crises and natural disasters, nuclear smuggling, proliferation of chemical and biological weapons, cyber-warfare, illegal migration, the spread of infectious disease, the global drug trade, illegal trafficking, and transnational crime. These problems constitute the "new security dilemma".[7] They transcend sovereign boundaries and cannot be resolved by one national military force defeating another. Maryann Cusimano argues that "even if organisation, training, and equipment priorities are changed to better prepare for the type of conflict that now predominates, military force is not well suited to these conflicts."[8] The new security dilemma – which involves a combination of military and other social, economic, environmental, and political dimensions – stands as a major challenge for the future of the military profession in all states, including Canada.

The new security dilemma also poses a major challenge to the principles underlying international law. An understanding of war as natural or inevitable, and the military as destined to warfare, is a dangerous obstacle to collective security and global peace. In the absence of authority higher than the state, international law sets out specific guidelines about how wars should be fought if avenues for peaceful conflict resolution fail. The doctrine of just war, for example, is a centuries-old legacy drawn from numerous European religious and secular sources.[9] Ideas about just war have been rendered increasingly problematic by the preponderance of intrastate conflicts in which "aggressor" and "victim" are not easy to identify and actors are not limited to states and national militaries. As a result of changes in conflict and insecurity, thinking about the appropriate roles and functions of the military needs a radical new vision.

THE POLICE

The police are an organized civil force. The role of police is to maintain order, prevent and detect crime, and enforce the law within a state. This means that police forces deal routinely with criminals in society. The modern era of policing is generally dated from Robert Peel's legislation in 1829 in England, which established principles for modern urban policing for the London Metropolitan Police Force. According to Peel, "The basic mission for which the police exist is to prevent crime and disorder as an alternative to the repression of crime and disorder by military force and severity of legal punishment".[10] The Metropolitan Police model competed with the paramilitary model of the Royal Irish Constabulary, often prevalent in British colonies.[11] Supporters of liberal democracy were uncomfortable with the paramilitary model and with the implication that police served those who ruled rather than serving the law. This, some argued, positioned police as a threat to political opposition and a potential menace to society as a whole.[12] As a reaction to this critique, policing services developed the democratic principles of public control and responsibility to the community.

Building on Sir John Moore's model of preventive military discipline[13] and the reforming philosophy of Jeremy Bentham, the British model emphasized prevention of crime over punishment and conviction.[14] British ideas about policing were adapted to the Canadian context, and thus provide insight into the evolution of the role of the Royal Canadian Mounted Police (RCMP). Although modelled on the paramilitary Royal Irish Constabulary, ideals of democratic policing emerged in Canadian urban centres.[15] The evolution is embodied in the motto of the Metropolitan Toronto Police Department: "To serve and protect".[16] In theory, the ideals of policing in Canada are to enhance the quality of democratic social life and to provide assistance during times of need. As a democratic society, Canada is cognizant of the need to balance the fundamental contradiction in policing. Police require social support and public respect in order to perform their functions effectively, but it is ultimately the responsibility of the police to enforce the law and maintain public order. Enforcement in democratic society involves the goal of social control, the basis for which is ultimately the use of force.[17]

Policing in Canada has undergone a transition from the crime-control model dominant in the 1960s to a more collaborative approach referred to in criminology as "community policing".[18] The RCMP defines community-based policing as:

> ...shared responsibility for problems and solutions between the police and members of the community to help them identify and solve their problems rather than simply target the symptoms. Partnerships are formed in a network format rather than hierarchical structure, with many agencies within the community, who all work together to ensure safe homes and safe communities.[19]

In one important respect, therefore, the military and police serve a common function in democratic society. They are entrusted with protecting a constituency while upholding order and punishing those who break the law. As they are conventionally understood, the military protects society from external threat, while the police protect society from internal threat. The external/internal axis that has traditionally divided the jurisdictions of the military and the police has been fundamentally obscured on account of new functions associated with peacekeeping and counter-terrorism policy.

CANADIAN PEACE-BUILDING AND HUMAN SECURITY

Canadians have long been active in international conflict resolution, with a reputation as impartial arbiters supporting a more equitable and stable world. As a result of the changing nature of international conflict in the 1990s, Canadian contributions to international conflict resolution efforts experienced two paradigm shifts. The first was a transition from peacekeeping to peace-building. The second was a parallel shift from national to human security.[20] The American-led war on terror then reversed some of the characteristics of these shifts.

The peace-building initiative draws from a history of human rights and development practices developed under international law and organizations, such as the United Nations and national development agencies.[21] The philosophy of conventional deterrence, i.e. containing, managing, or moderating hostilities through the threat to use military force, has been replaced in Canadian foreign policy by international conflict-resolution efforts based on the notion of peace-building rather than peacekeeping. Peace-building is an effort to respond to the more complex nature of current missions of Canadian armed forces in war-torn societies. The strategy promoted by peace-building is proactive in attempting to address the root causes of conflict in addition to reacting to the immediate crisis.[22] Canadian efforts to prevent a renewal of hostilities in conflict zones have extended far beyond cease-fire agreements between states, to such activities as institution-building, observing elections, and supporting democratic transitions. Peace-building has also focussed on empowerment of civil society, inter-communal cooperation, and the promotion of long-term stability in ethnically divided societies. In short, peace-building is "the effort to strengthen the prospects for internal peace and decrease the likelihood of violent conflict.... to enhance the indigenous capacity of a society to manage conflict without violence".[23] Local communities, moderate leaderships, NGOs, youth, and women are encouraged to contribute to the peaceful resolution of conflict through cooperation and capacity-building.

Peace-building involves a parallel transition from national security to a human-security agenda. Human security shifts the focus from states as the primary actors of international affairs, to human beings, with individuals and their communities, rather than states and national boundaries, as the central points of reference for global peace and security. The main objective of human security is to broaden the agenda of security by including non-military issues such as human rights, sustainable development, gender equality, cultural diversity, and protection of the environment.[24]

Both the military and the police have contributions to make towards peace-building and human security. However, adapting to the needs of current missions requires a reorientation of institutional goals, skills, and expertise for both. In essence, peace-building blurs task distinctions between the police and military forces.[25] Civilian experts make important contributions to peacekeeping operations.[26] Some would argue that the participation of non-military actors promotes the human-security ideal of democratizing foreign policy through broader representation of Canadian society in the execution of foreign policy.

Police forces trained for law enforcement and crime prevention are well suited to intervention in intrastate conflicts. Indeed, peacekeeping and peace-building deal with crime prevention on a global scale, and crime is more prevalent in societies undergoing conflict.[27] The Canadian community-policing model is well suited to restoring order in conflict zones as democratic institutions and civil society are being developed. The RCMP and other Canadian police forces have been instrumental in training, reforming, professionalizing, and democratizing foreign police services in peace-support missions in post-conflict situations. In addition, in missions ranging from Rwanda and Sierra Leone to Kosovo and East Timor, Canadian police have been involved in investigating war crimes, human rights violations, and small-arms trafficking.[28]

Canadian civilians have increased their participation in some activities abroad that have hitherto been the exclusive preserve of the military. The Canadian Forces have always been involved in operations other than fighting wars. Search and rescue operations, disaster relief, humanitarian assistance, territorial surveillance for prevention of illegal activities such as drug or weapons trafficking, and institution-building increasingly involve policing roles in foreign societies.[29] Policing is a complicated task that requires sensitivity to the collective identities and enmities of the population being policed. The changing roles of the military and police in contemporary international affairs have affected our understanding of the boundaries between their activities.

An important dilemma accompanies the transformation of peacekeeping missions. The proposal by the Secretary-General of the UN for peace-enforcement units implies more heavily armed troops who might be involved directly in combat.[30] Beyond possible war-fighting, enforcement still implies an international policing function since it involves intervention within states. Heavily armed peacekeepers with a policing function render problematic the original claim of UN forces to be impartial arbiters between parties to a conflict. Enforcement impedes consensual alliances with civil society groups, which are necessary for political, social, economic, and other tasks. Indeed, the idea of enforcement has not gained widespread support, and the 1995 Supplement to the Secretary-General's *Agenda for Peace* is less assertive on the subject than the original document was in 1993.

CANADIAN COUNTER-TERRORISM

After the shifts in the 1990s from peacekeeping to peace-building and from national to human security, the subsequent shift in Canadian security policy in 2001 resulted directly from the terrorist attacks on the United States on 11 September 2001. Canada's most significant responses to these attacks occurred in the military, legislative, and policing arenas. In the military sphere, Canada launched Operation APOLLO. Immediately following the attacks and with very little public debate, Canada took action to support the U.S.-led campaign against the Taliban regime in Afghanistan. With the exception of its commitment to humanitarian assistance, Canadian action coincided with the predominantly military response of the United States. The war on terrorism contrasts with the movement of the human-security agenda away from military responses to violence.

In the legislative sphere, the Government of Canada introduced Bill C-36 in the House of Commons on 15 October 2001. Bill C-36, the *Anti-Terrorism Act*, offered a package of sweeping legislative measures, which "takes aim at terrorist organisations and strengthens investigation, prosecution and prevention of terrorist activities at home and abroad".[31] The Act aimed to prevent terrorists from entering Canada, protecting Canadians from terrorist acts, and thereby providing the tools to identify, prosecute, convict, and punish terrorists.[32] As in the military sphere, Canada's legislative response to terrorism was largely punitive. With the exception of a vague acknowledgement of the underlying causes for terrorism and the need to address them, the focus of legislation was to criminalize activities associated with terrorism. The package did include a set of checks and balances to ensure that anti-terrorism legislation would be consistent with Canada's legal system, particularly the *Charter of Rights and Freedoms*. However, Operation APOLLO and Bill C-36 establish clear boundaries for fighting terrorism by seeking to capture and punish the enemy whether at home or abroad in a manner that raises a number of important questions about the democratic process.

Liberal democracies face a dilemma when responding to terrorism. Since democratic governments depend on electoral support, they must maintain order and stability while preserving democratic institutions and ways of life. Democracies ensure rights and freedoms in pursuit of personal goals. If citizens disagree with government policy, a certain level of civil disobedience and political protest is tolerated, and even encouraged, to contribute to public debate and to permit the public to influence policy. However, during counter-terrorism campaigns, states infringe more heavily on their citizens and require that individuals and groups cede a degree of their freedom. This may involve a more assertive role for police forces and intelligence services. Democratic states must mobilize public support to maintain legitimacy during counter-terrorism campaigns, especially if the campaign against terrorism extends over a long period of time.

Three main government agencies deal with terrorist threats to public safety: law enforcement, the criminal justice system, and intelligence services. These agencies must cooperate and coordinate their policies during counter-terrorism campaigns. The need for cooperation generally results in the centralization of command-and-control measures and a substantial degree of information.

Legislation defines terrorism in democracies. The fight against terrorism is analogous to the fight against other violent offences: both are considered threats to public safety and the rule of law. It is the responsibility of the legal system to determine what activities constitute terrorism. Conventional definitions of terrorism differentiate between terrorist and criminal activity.[33] While both terrorists and ordinary criminals employ violence to achieve a particular goal, their motivations differ. Terrorism is motivated by political goals that would serve a broader constituency, such as transforming society, ending colonial rule, or struggling for national liberation. Criminals, on the other hand, are motivated by self-interest, usually material profit from theft, fraud, bribery, or murder. Criminal activity is self-contained because it is not intended to have consequences beyond the immediate act. Once the profit is made, the criminal is satisfied. Terrorists may perpetrate the same acts as ordinary criminals, but their objective is for the act to have a wider impact, whether it is psychological intimidation of a target society or ultimately the desired political change. The terrorist supports a cause used to justify the means employed.

Some anti-terrorist laws aim at prevention by addressing the underlying causes of terrorist activity. Poverty and alienation may breed violence which leads to terrorist activity. Other anti-terrorist measures are punitive, aiming to deter terrorists with severe penalties. Punitive laws provide police with powers needed to apprehend and charge those who commit terrorist acts. Other legislation may have symbolic or psychological effects, "expressing public revulsion at particular outrages and reassuring the public that something is being done".[34]

Once legislation concerning terrorist activity is in place, the task of implementing the law falls to the police services. The criminalization of terrorism provides police with a clear basis for action using police tools. Generally, a package of counter-terrorist measures provides the police with more authority and autonomy to do their work effectively.[35] Emergency legislation can allow the police to use extraordinary measures for the surveillance and apprehension of suspects. For example, although terrorism has always been considered a serious criminal offence in Canada, the new *Anti-Terrorism Act* is the first to define terrorism and terrorist-related activities as criminal offences. Previously, the application of other criminal codes was particularly problematic in attempts to link to terrorism such activities as facilitating, providing skills, procurement, harbouring, funding, and other criminal acts. As a result, the Act has given law enforcement agencies a broad mandate to pursue their work proactively with such tools as investigative hearings and preventive arrests to facilitate their pursuit of terrorists.[36]

Intelligence services play a role in counter-terrorist activity. According to Paul Wilkinson, "The secret of winning the battle against terrorism in an open democratic society is winning the intelligence war."[37] To prevent terrorism, liberal democracies have different types of intelligence services, some of which operate internationally while others are limited to operations within their own borders. The role of intelligence services is to monitor evolving threats to the security interests of their country, investigate activities, and report to their respective governments. Intelligence services assess a wide variety of threats to national security, including clandestine or intelligence activities of foreign governments and actions affecting social, political, and economic institutions, infrastructure, and communications systems. Although intelligence agencies are responsible to civil authority, they must operate with some secrecy. Much of the information generated by intelligence services is not subject to public scrutiny, and secretive methods sit uneasily with democratic rights.

Counter-terrorism in liberal democratic countries treads a precarious path between punitive and democratic elements. Wilkinson points out the risks posed by emergency anti-terrorist legislation for democratic systems. The deliberate suspension or limitation of civil liberties on the grounds of expediency over the long term may result in the erosion of civil liberties and may even play into the hands of terrorists by increasing the anger of their potential recruits. Police must act within the law in order to uphold public confidence and respect for the criminal justice system. Wilkinson suggests three safeguards to preserve civil liberties and rule of law during the fight against terrorism. (1) Anti-terrorism policy and its implementation should be democratically accountable and thus should remain under the control of civil authority. (2) Government and security services must conduct their anti-terrorist activities within the law, ensuring that the normal legal process is preserved and that those suspected of terrorist activity are charged and tried before the courts of law. (3) Finally, emergency legislation should be approved by the legislature only for a fixed and limited period and should be subject to review, published as widely as possible, and administered impartially.[38]

Some dilemmas arise when intelligence services and police forces cooperate in counter-terrorism policy. The role of the police is to seek prosecution, while the role of intelligence services is to accumulate information. Because intelligence services want information to continue to flow, they do not want people arrested and taken out of circulation. This raises two problems. First, it may leave potentially dangerous criminals on the streets. Second, if criminals know they are being watched, their activities become more clandestine. Prosecuting a suspect for a lesser offence, such as money laundering (a criminal offence under anti-terrorist legislation), may complicate the investigation of a more serious terrorist action.[39] However, closer contact with the community and involvement in local activities allow the police better access to law enforcement intelligence that may relate to support such as funding and harbouring terrorists. If police information can be shared in ways that promote the objectives of the military, the intelligence services, and the police, such an integrated approach is the most effective way of protecting society from crime, whether that crime is motivated by politics or profit.

SUMMING UP

This chapter has argued that new forms of conflict and insecurity demand reconsideration of the roles of Canadian military and police forces. The nature of conflict and humanitarian intervention is different in intrastate conflicts than in wars between states. As a result, conventional definitions of the roles, functions, organization, and training of military and police forces need revision. As traditionally understood, the military defends the state from external threat, while the police protect society from internal threat. Ultimately, both the military and the police are institutions designed to safeguard democratic society and the rule of law, both within the state and in the international system.

Conventional understanding of the civilian-military division of labour has changed in recent years. The military have performed more tasks associated with civilians, and the police are part of a growing civilian component of military operations. Some might argue that this blurring of functions constitutes a democratization of foreign policy, one of the main goals of the human security agenda. However, it is appropriate to ask whether the blurring of distinctions is merely a pretext for transferring costs at a time of reduced military spending.

It is obvious that the military and police must work together to be effective in foreign interventions and counter-terrorism campaigns. This requires different training regimens and preparedness for everyone involved. Both the military and the police systems depend on coercive and punitive powers; although force is not always necessary, the capacity to threaten or use force is a source of power and influence. Both the move towards enforcement in the 1990s and the U.S.-led war against terrorism since September 11 have focussed on power and punishment. As a result, both policy shifts have generated opposition in some sectors of society that do not trust the military and police. Police and military forces alike must never forget that serving and protecting society must always be synonymous with the goals of the democratic process.

NOTES

1. Many thanks to the Canadian Forces Leadership Institute for its generous funding towards presentation of this paper at the IUS Conference in Kingston, Ontario, on 26–27 October 2002.
2. Carl von Clausewitz, *On War* (London: Routledge and Kegan, 1968).
3. Charles W. Kegley, Jr. and Eugene R. Wittkopf, *World Politics: Trend and Transformation* (New York: St. Martin's/Worth, 1999), 403.
4. Ted Robert Gurr, "Why Minorities Rebel: A global analysis of communal mobilization and conflict since 1945," *International Political Science Review*, 14:2 (1993): 161–201.

5. Cees De Rover, "A New Interest for Human Rights and Humanitarian Law," *International Review of the Red Cross*, no. 835 (1999): 637.

6. Jonathan R. White, *Terrorism: An Introduction* (Belmont: West/Wadsworth, 1998), 8.

7. Maryann K. Cusimano, *Beyond Sovereignty: Issues for a Global Agenda* (New York: Bedford/St. Martin's, 2000).

8. Ibid., 33.

9. Simon Chesterman, *Just War or Just Peace? Humanitarian Intervention and International Law* (Oxford: Oxford University Press, 2001) and Jean Bethke Elshtain, ed., *Just War Theory* (New York: New York University Press, 1992).

10. Dennis Forcese, *Policing Canadian Society* (Scarborough, ON: Prentice Hall Allyn and Bacon Canada, 1999), 3.

11. Charles Reith, *A New Study of Police History* (Edinburgh: Oliver and Boyd, 1956) and David M. Anderson and David Killingray, eds., *Policing the Empire: Government, Authority and Control, 1830-1940* (New York: Manchester University Press, 1991).

12. Tony Jefferson, *The Case Against Paramilitary Policing* (Milton Keynes: Open University Press, 1990).

13. Reith, *New Study of Police History*, 112-120.

14. John Sewell, *Police: Urban Policing in Canada* (Toronto: James, Lorimer and Company, 1985), 26.

15. William Baker, ed., *The Mounted Police and Prairie Society, 1873-1919*. Series: Canadian Plains Studies (Regina: Canadian Plains Research Center, 1998). In Canada, community policing took root despite the paramilitary origins of the RCMP, but it did so in urban European communities, while the paramilitary policing model continued to prevail in rural areas and in the policing of native and immigrant populations.

16. Lorne Tepperman, *Crime Control* (Toronto: McGraw-Hill Ryerson, 1977), 29.

17. Forcese, *Policing Canadian Society*, 2.

18. Forcese, *Policing Canadian Society*. See also Dennis Jay Kenney and Robert P. McNamara, *Police and Policing: Contemporary Issues* (Westport, CT: Praeger, 1999) and Paul Palango, *The Last Guardians: The Crisis in the RCMP – and in Canada* (Toronto: McClelland and Stewart, 1998).

19. *RCMP Peacekeeping Annual Review 2001-2002* (Ottawa: Public Works Canada, 2001), 26.

20. Carolyn M. Stephenson, "Peacekeeping and Peacemaking," in Michael T. Snarr and D. Neil Snarr, eds., *Introducing Global Issues* (Boulder, CO: Lynne Rienner, 1998), 65.

21. Department of Foreign Affairs and International Trade, *Human Security: Safety for People in a Changing World* (Ottawa: Public Works Canada, April 1999). See also Heather Owens and Barbara Arneil, "The Human Security Paradigm Shift: A New Lens on Canadian Foreign Policy?", *Canadian Foreign Policy*, vol. 7, no. 1 (Fall 1999): 1–12, and Paul Heinbecker, "Human Security," *Canadian Foreign Policy*, vol. 7, no. 1 (Fall 1999): 19–25.

22. Hay, 1999.

23. Department of Foreign Affairs and International Trade and Canadian International Development Agency, *The Strategic Framework for Canadian Peacebuilding Activities* (Ottawa: Public Works Canada, 1997).

24. Department of Foreign Affairs and International Trade, *Human Security*.

25. De Rover, "New Interest for Human Rights and Humanitarian Law," 637.

26. Parkinson quoted by Michael Small, "Peacebuilding in Postconflict Societies" in Rob McRae and Don Hubert, eds., *Human Security and the New Diplomacy: Protecting People, Promoting Peace* (Montreal: McGill-Queen's University Press, 2001).

27. "RCMP Directional Statement 2000," *Gazette*, vol. 62, no. 1 (2000), 3.

28. *RCMP Peacekeeping 2000-2001 Annual Review* (Ottawa: Public Works Canada, 2001), 12.

29. *A Wake Up Call for Canada: The Need for a New Military* (Toronto: The Royal Canadian Military Institute, 2001), 12.

30. Report of the Secretary-General on the Work of the Organization, *Supplement to an Agenda for Peace,* Position Paper of the Secretary-General on the Occasion of the Fiftieth Anniversary of the United Nations, A/50/60 – S/1995/1 (New York: United Nations, 3 January 1995), paragraph 77.

31. Department of Justice, "Anti-Terrorism Act Receives Royal Assent," December 18, 2001, http://canada.justice.gc.ca/en/news/nr/2001/doc_28215.html/

32. Department of Justice, "Government of Canada Introduces Anti-Terrorism Act," http://canada.justice.gc.ca/en/news/nr/2001/doc_27785.html/

33. David J. Whittaker, *The Terrorism Reader* (Routledge: London and New York, 2001).

34. Paul Wilkinson, *Terrorism Versus Democracy: The Liberal State Response* (London: Frank Cass, 2000), 113.

35. Interview with J. Wayne Pilgrim, Superintendent, OIC National Security Investigations Branch, Criminal Intelligence Directorate, RCMP, on 2 May 2002 in Ottawa.

36. Interview with representatives of the Department of Justice on 1 May 2002 in Ottawa.

37. Wilkinson, *Terrorism Versus Democracy*, p. 95.

38. Ibid.

39. Interview with Alistair Hensler, former Deputy Director of Operations, CSIS, on 3 May 2002 in Ottawa.

Changing Culture and Values

six

Social Capital
The Currency of the Armed Forces

Ulrich vom Hagen[1]

Over the last few years, the disciplines of sociology and political science, as well as a more general political discourse
in Germany and the U.S., have adopted a fashionable new term
that repeatedly surfaces in debates over the present and the future
of Western societies: *social capital*. Its usage presupposes that social capital plays a decisive role wherever social relations, social
trust, solidarity, moral norms, or even the efficiency of administrative and political systems is in question. Therefore, the success
of the term does not come as much of a surprise, since it deals with
the fundamental question of what keeps modern societies together.
The concept of social capital is therefore central to our understanding of how military forces adapt to social and cultural change.

A hundred years ago, the eminent German sociologist Max
Weber was already quite pessimistic about the prospects for the
values that contribute to social cohesion surviving the transformation from traditional to modern societies.[2] Today, the discussion
concerns whether highly individualistic, post-modern societies can
be integrated at all.[3] How much altruism, solidarity, and cooperation does a society need in order to maintain a balance
between individual interest and public interest? The term *social
interest* serves as a framework that promises to keep the tension
between individualism and societal morale alive.

What is surprising about the current debate in the U.S. and
Germany is the fact that it takes place with apparent disregard for
the active and complicated debate about social capital coming out
of France. In fact, this debate has simply been ignored, although it

has thoroughly shaped academic and political discussion in France for decades. It is striking that the debate in France gave social capital a different meaning, although it, too, is about social relations, solidarity, and mutual trust. The French discourse also has a deeply critical ethos. It calls into question the systems of official self-promotion and self-justification of modern societies, which make individual success and performance the only legitimate measures for the distribution of social status.[4] In France, social capital describes the network of relations that contribute to the production and reproduction of social inequality and ensure that career chances and resources of power not only are based on performance and qualification but, beyond that, are also based on coming from the "right" social background. Thus the French social capital discourse helps us to understand, for example, why officers tend to come from a common social background.

These two discourses are associated with the names of two prominent academics: the American political scientist Robert D. Putnam and the French sociologist Pierre Bourdieu. Bourdieu systematically developed the term *capital social* in the 1970s; it has subsequently become part of a general vocabulary in the French education system. Likewise, Putnam's studies regarding social capital in the U.S. enjoyed immense success in the 1990s and have made him the best-known communitarian.[5]

'"SOCIAL CAPITAL" – THE AMERICAN DISCOURSE

Putnam's notion of social capital contains three elements. The first is *social trust*, which facilitates the social co-ordination required for co-operation between individuals. An example is an employee's trust that the employer will pay wages at the end of the month. The second is the *norm of generalized reciprocity*, which contributes to the solution of social dilemmas. For example, we are nice to people who are nice to us. The third element is *networks of civil-societal engagements*, which support generalized reciprocal norms and develop social trust. Political parties and officers' messes are examples of these networks.[6] With these central assumptions, Putnam refers both to classical theories of democracy and to transaction theories of economic approaches. He considers *civic associations* to be "foundations" and "schools of democracy". It is within civic associations that we develop social trust, which subsequently extends to generalized trust in other social fields. At the centre of Putnam's theory are the *traditional civic associations* – such as small local sports organizations, church groups and so on – out of which identification and solidarity are built. In an active social role, we learn to understand virtue and relationships. This understanding allows better communication, cooperation, and social trust outside of these associations. This is how social capital is generated and regenerated.

Putnam attempts to prove that social capital in the U.S. has eroded since the 1960s. He uses sequential comparisons to describe the social relations of the American citizen in the context of civil engagement and membership in organizations, through to personal relationships. He summarizes what he calls "America's declining social capital" in the pointed expression "bowling alone", the title of a 1995 essay, and the more optimistically entitled *Bowling Alone: The collapse and revival of American community*.[7] He pinpoints the principal cause of this social disenfranchisement as the "uncivic generation" of the baby boom. Although Putnam attempts to minimize the lamenting tone about "loss of community" in the U.S., the moralizing critique of individualism and the glorification of community remain nonetheless clear.[8]

CAPITAL SOCIAL – THE FRENCH DISCOURSE

In France, the term *capital social* is an integral part of a broad public discourse regarding social inequality. The groundwork for this concept was done by Pierre Bourdieu, whose social theory became widely known through his analysis of French society in the 1970s and '80s. Bourdieu's themes are the mechanisms for the production and reproduction of social structures within various social practices. To analyze these mechanisms, Bourdieu introduced the concept of the three types of capital in "the social world of economies".[9] Aside from *economic capital*, which is clearly the most meaningful form of material wealth (money or possession of real estate, for example), Bourdieu identifies *cultural capital* in three forms: In *incorporated form*, cultural capital is acquired through education. In *objectified form*, it is manifested through cultural goods (books, works of art, etc.). In its *institutionalized form*, cultural capital finds expression in proofs of legitimacy, such as academic certificates and titles. A staff college or military academy clearly embodies all three forms of cultural capital. Finally, *social capital* is:

the totality of real and potential resources which are related to the possession of a permanent network of more or less institutionalised *relations* and
mutual recognition; or, to put it otherwise, it is about resources, whose acces-
sibility is based in group-affiliation.[10]

Bourdieu conceives social capital, not as Putnam does in terms
of its collective value to societies, but as an *individual resource*. He
conceives this resource as an independent kind of capital, one that
arises empirically only in concert with the two other forms of capital. *Social capital* exerts a multiplier effect on available *economic*
and *cultural capital*. It functions, therefore, in relation to the un-
equal distribution of these forms of capital and thereby reinforces
the production and reproduction of social inequality. In other
words, individuals who have wealth, power, education, and status
also have the social capital that gives them an advantage over those
less well-placed in society, and the people they associate with have
similar advantages.[11] Bourdieu attempts to describe the rules that
determine how one form of capital is transformed into another:[12]
to "determine laws, according to which various forms of capital
(or, what amounts to the same thing, various forms of power) are
mutually transformed into each another".[13]

To understand the relationship between different forms of capital, Bourdieu develops an empirical *model of social space* oriented
around forms of capital rather than social class structures.[14]
Bourdieu's model accounts for a particular social position through
the volume of capital that one possesses, the forms of available
capital, and one's social career. Parallel with this concept of *social
space* is what Bourdieu calls the *space of life-style*, registering the
significance of everyday practices and symbolic life-style. According to Bourdieu's empirical studies, particular social positions are
organized according to these two *spaces*. Bourdieu clarifies the
agreement between the two spaces with his notion of *habitus*. For
example, an educated middle-class professional develops by habit certain practices and ways of representing herself that become thoroughly
internalized. These habits then condition her social relationships with
men and women in other social and lifestyle spaces.

Bourdieu's concept of social capital may be the most theoretically refined,[15] but even Putnam has recently suggested that "social
capital might have antisocial effects", by which he means that it
might undermine community.[16] Putnam thus differentiates between the inclusive and exclusive dimensions of social capital: "Of
all the dimensions along which forms of social capital vary, perhaps

the most important is the distinction between *bridging* (or inclusive) and *bonding* (or exclusive)".[17] In both cases, solidarity and readiness to help are not universal but are limited to smaller communities, understood as traditional or rationally motivated forms of support. Above all, however, Putnam poses the normative question as to "how the positive consequences of social capital – mutual support, cooperation, trust, institutional effectiveness – can be maximised, and the negative manifestations – sectarianism, ethnocentrism, corruption – minimised".[18]

Bridging social capital is Putnam's key concept for discussing the positive effects of social capital. However, his attempt to describe how it is generated and how it works is not very convincing. He seems to be looking for an optimistic interpretation of social inequality, rather than analyzing its complexity. His theoretical differentiation of social capital into two extreme poles (*bridging* and *bonding*) does not seem to match complex reality. In comparison with Bourdieu's elaborate notion of social capital, three weaknesses in Putnam's theory stand out. The first is his confusion of the causes and effects of social capital, a confusion which results in a kind of circular argumentation. The second is the unconvincing extension of the notion of social capital to certain regions and to states. Thirdly, Putnam's idealization of the positive effects of social capital requires a thorough disregard for its negative effects. Putnam simplistically reduces social capital to its association with democracy and collective good health.

Approaches that conceive of social capital as an *individual resource* seem to be theoretically and empirically superior to those that understand it as a collective value of societies. Bourdieu presents a discourse that refers to *bonding solidarity*. This has its origin in Marx's description of *class consciousness*. For example, Bourdieu demonstrates that France's elite has informal and institutional networks at its disposal to an extent unmatched by any other system of elites in the West.[19] Decisive here are the associations of the *anciens élèves* of the *Grandes écoles*, particularly the institutional connections among the elite colleges and the elite institutions of public management, the so-called *Grands corps d'État*. The homogeneous, self-reproducing elite are sustained by a high level of *esprit de corps*, a practically identical development within the educational system, and a similar bourgeois background. Their social capital is manifested not only through their obligation to maintain solidarity and support within their own class but also through exclusion of those who do not belong.

SOCIAL CAPITAL – THE CURRENCY OF THE ARMED FORCES

Bourdieu analyzes social capital in terms of diverse *social fields* that range from the religious to the academic. The number of social fields for analysis remains virtually unlimited, since social fields always arise where there is a struggle for recognition, power, and status. The military can be understood as just such a social field, in which and for which representatives from various camps struggle against one another. My research arises from the sense that civil-military relations can be understood better if we conceive of the military *as* a social system with its own norms and rules, rather than as an organization in relation *to* a social system. Bourdieu's concept of social capital is relevant to military sociology, which has to address the specific military ethic and structures expressed as *military culture*.

The theme of military culture has been the topic of much discussion recently. It is my sense that a military-sociological research programme has much to learn from Bourdieu's method. An important task is to clarify the mechanisms through which military culture is produced and reproduced. Is military culture inconsistent with the culture of the general population? Informed work on military culture seems to be a precondition for understanding the so-called *civil-military gap*. At a practical level, there is the question of public accountability. The structures of identification and command within the military are perceived by the public to be associated with patriarchal, oppressive, and freedom-limiting values. An increasingly wary public and political culture is highly resistant to notions of hierarchy and authoritarianism. How do military institutions communicate the necessity of values typically associated with a highly conservative attitude – for example, loyalty, discipline, rigour, collectivism, even the readiness to exercise violence – to a culture that is so thoroughly defined by the values of possessive individualism, tolerance, pluralism, and non-patriarchal forms of organisation? I am not attempting to answer this question here, merely to advocate a more nuanced understanding of why and how citizens become soldiers, how rule and power in the military are legitimized, and what makes soldiers professional. We need an alternative to the rather outdated and despairing notion that soldiers are simply the product of a set of dehumanizing techniques designed only to produce fodder for a war machine.

We might begin to better understand military culture through an analysis of the institutional practices through which officers' careers are initially determined and continuously formed until retirement. This kind of social determination and the constant pressure to compete, even independent of any conscious process of selection, guarantees the long-term coherency of the officer corps. Thus one must study the relations between the objective characteristics of the military institution (such as ranks, units, and activities) and the socially constituted dispositions of military personnel (such as values, attitudes, and norms) as they interact within the institution. These relations are expressed in Bourdieu's central concept of *habitus*. *Habitus* mediates between social position on the one hand and the actions, preferences, ways of cognition, and decisions of individuals on the other. It manifests itself in the form of gestures, mimicry, language, and taste. Bourdieu contends that social systems are enacted by their members, not simply imposed from above as a structure of power. Thus it is important that officers express solidarity, cohesion, and conformism, not simply by following orders but rather by embodying these values, expressed in a specific *habitus*. The *habitus* of soldiers is a cultural competence acquired in a homogeneous group. In this context, interpersonal relations are more than the relationship of one individual to another. The truth of an interaction is never to be found in itself alone, but in social structures outside the particular situation. It is in this sense that Bourdieu helps us to think about the very notion of *esprit de corps*, not as some ideological concept that is forcibly imposed but rather as something that is expressed through the willingness of the corporate body.

How is social capital generated? What qualities must one have in order to benefit from it? In the case of the military, these qualities centre around behaviour that reflects conformism, a conservative attitude, and readiness to perform. Cultivating these characteristics has a complicated relationship to the social background in which they arise. Officers generally choose their profession with the intent of leaving behind their lower-middle- or middle-class family background.[20] In so doing, they bring to the modern military profession precisely these petit-bourgeois values of conformism, political conservatism, and readiness to perform. This is part of a dialectical relationship between the social structures of society and representation of these social structures within the military. Above all, relationships and contacts with other career officers play an enormous role in maintaining and reproducing the military system.

SUMMING UP

The term *social capital* became quite popular in the sociological discourse of the 1990s. The heated question in North America was what holds society together. Social capital was used in the context of social relations, social trust, solidarity, and morale. In France, attention was drawn to questions of power and its distribution within societies. This more critical approach raises questions concerning the distribution and reproduction of status and social imbalance. The concept of social capital can assist with a better understanding of the processes and interactions within the military institution, by creating a richer theory within which to consider military culture. The ways in which social structures are produced and reproduced are not restricted to civilian society, but are found within the military just as in any other institution. Social networks are the places where such processes occur, because they offer acknowledgement and trusting relationships. We can understand the social practices and the actions of individuals only if we realize what is behind them. Depending on social position and resources, an individual in a social network has different options. In order to define *resource* more precisely, I referred to Bourdieu's theory of types of capital (economic capital, social capital, and cultural capital). Constant bargaining about the worth of each type of capital is part of social processes in general.

Bourdieu's concept of *habitus* helps to explain how objective structures and subjective action determine each other. *Habitus* is a theoretical construct, but it has empirical manifestations in the way we do things within a group. The *habitus* approach might allow us to better understand "the logic of appropriateness"[21] within the military as an institution. Social capital is the totality of actual and potential resources, which are connected with more or less institutionalized ways of knowing and respecting each other. Social capital should be understood as a resource that is connected with membership in a group. The phenomenon is well known, for example, in military regiments or units where relationships and contacts are very valuable. Treating social capital as the currency of the armed forces might help us to understand military culture better.

NOTES

1. I would like to thank my wife Sarah for her help in polishing the English version of this text and for her comments on this paper.
2. M. Weber, *Gesammelte Aufsätze zur Soziologie und Sozialpolitik*, Tübingen, 1988, 414.
3. U. Beck and E. Beck-Gernsheim, "Individualisierung in modernen Gesellschaften – Perspektiven und Kontroversen in Subjektorientierten Soziologie," in *Riskante Freiheiten*, U. Beck and E. Beck-Gernsheim, eds. (Frankfurt/Main, 1994), 33.
4. C. Offe, "Leistungsprinzip und industrielle Arbeit, Mechanismen der Statusverteilung in Arbeitsorganisation der Industriellen" (Leistungsgesellschaft: Frankfurt/Main, 1973): 7.
5. In the past decade, many other academics have worked with the term *social capital*. Coleman and Fukuyama are two who have not received as much attention as Bourdieu or Putnam. J. S. Coleman, "Social Capital in Creation of Human Capital," *American Journal of Sociology* 94 (1988): 95-121; J. S. Coleman, *Foundations of Modern Society* (Cambridge, 1990); F. Fukuyama, *Trust: The social virtues and the creation of prosperity* (New York, 1995).
6. R. D. Putnam, R. Leonardi, and R. Nanetti, *Making Democracy Work: Civic Traditions in Modern Italy* (Princeton, NJ: 1993), 170; R. D. Putnam, "Bowling Alone: America's declining social capital," *Journal of Democracy* 6 (1995): 35-42.
7. Putnam, "Bowling Alone: America's declining social capital"; R. D. Putnam, *Bowling Alone: The collapse and revival of American community* (New York, 2000).
8. Putnam, *Bowling Alone: The collapse and revival of American community*, 75
9. P. Bourdieu, "Ökonomisches Kapital, kulturelles Kapital, soziales Kapital," in *Soziale Ungleichheiten*, R. Kreckel, ed. (Göttingen: Sonderband 2 der Sozialen Welt, 1983), 183–198.
10. Bourdieu, "Ökonomisches Kapital, kulturelles Kapital, soziales Kapital," 190f.
11. "The scope of social capital which the individual possesses (...) depends as much on how wide his own network of relations is, as it does on the extent of (...) capital possessed by those with whom he is in relation" (ibid., 191).
12. "general science of the economy of praxis" (ibid., 51)
13. Bourdieu, "Ökonomisches Kapital, kulturelles Kapital, soziales Kapital," 184.
14. P. Bourdieu, "Die feinen Unterschiede," *Kritik der gesellschaftlichen Urteilskraft* (Frankfurt/Main: 1996): 171ff.
15. A. Portes, "Social Capital: Its Origins and Applications in Modern Sociology," *Annual Reviews of Sociology* 24 (1998): 1–24.
16. Putnam, *Bowling Alone: The collapse and revival of American community*, 446.
17. Ibid., 22.
18. Ibid., 446.
19. P. Bourdieu, *La Noblesse d'Etat: Grandes écoles et esprit du corps* (Paris: 1989).
20. A. Bonnemann and C. Posner, "Die politischen Orientierungen der Studenten an den Universitäten der Bundeswehr im Vergleich zu den Studenten an öffentlichen Hochschulen," *Sicherheit und Frieden* 1 (2002).
21. J.G. March and J.P. Olson, *Rediscovering Institutions. The Organizational Basis of Politics* (New York and London: 1989).

seven

Turkish National Security Doctrine and Democratization in the New Security Environment

Gökhan Yücel

Security is development and without development there can be no security.[1]

Robert McNamara

Turkish Youth! Your first duty is forever to preserve and to defend the Turkish Independence and the Turkish Republic...This is the very foundation of your existence and your future. This foundation is your most precious treasure. In the future, too, there may be malevolent people at home and abroad who will wish to deprive you of this treasure. If some day you are compelled to defend your independence and your republic, you must not tarry to weigh the possibilities and circumstances of the situation before taking up your duty... Furthermore, they may identify their personal interests with the political designs of the invaders. The country may be impoverished, ruined and exhausted... You will find the strength you need in your noble blood.[2]

Mustafa Kemal Ataturk, His Address to the Turkish Youth

On 4 August 2001 Deputy Prime Minister Mesut Yilmaz addressed the Motherland Party (ANAP) Congress about contentious issues that had never been treated so bluntly. Speaking about political and economic development, he focussed on the most sensitive issue in Turkish political life: national security.[3] He touched upon Turkey's current security dilemma, ethnic and political issues, and growing regime disputes. He admitted that security measures occasionally violate human rights and emphasized the close link between violation of civil liberties and Turkey's low democratic standards. He argued that this has damaged the economy and has caused loss of human and economic capital, crumbling state services, and a decline in public order. Most importantly, he stressed that escalating tensions with the European Union over Turkey's democratic record might prove catastrophic to Turkey's economic aspirations. Is Turkey ready, he asked, to pay the full cost of entering the European Union? Is there an ideological and pragmatic consensus at both the elite and the popular levels that favours integration with Europe? Although Yilmaz is enthusiastic about EU membership, he sees the "national security syndrome" as a serious obstacle:

> ... National security is an essential paradigm that ultimately aims to preserve the state. Yet the application of this concept in today's Turkey seems to work quite the contrary. The term "national security" has become a barrier that thwarts every single step to enhance the future of this country. Turkey might be the only country which uses such a term to cut the vital veins of the state ... The key to change is hidden in the term "national security". It has been impossible to take steps to consolidate the survival and improve the welfare of our state because of the concept of national security. If Turkey wants to make progress, it has to overcome the national security syndrome. The content and circumstances of national security should be opened to public debate. The true key to turning our face to Europe, and hence to change, is to redefine the limits and boundaries of national security. National security concerns the whole nation, and so the nation should be concerned with it.[4]

This chapter analyzes the interplay between Turkish national security doctrine and democratization in the new security environment, with particular attention to Turkey's EU candidacy. By describing the public debate that followed Yilmaz's contentious statement, I will illustrate the different interpretations of the term "national security". Did the shock of the speech sufficiently undermine orthodox thinking to establish the conditions for democratization?[5] I will then summarize the Turkish national security concept on the basis of two seminal documents: the National Security Policy Document and the Ministry of Defence White Paper. Discussing the official policy and the military role allows us to identify the social and political gap that creates what Yilmaz calls the "national security syndrome" in civil society debates.[6]

THE PUBLIC DEBATE OVER THE "NATIONAL SECURITY SYNDROME"

Mesut Yilmaz did not start a new debate by attacking the ethos of national security. In the 1990s he claimed to distinguish between spheres of national security appropriate for military and government scrutiny. The Turkish General Staff (TGS) had cautioned that no one should confuse the determination to fight separatist or fundamentalist activities with their personal ambitions.[7] The TGS response to Yilmaz's April speech came in a press release on 7 August 2001, which stated that matters related to the existence, well-being, and prosperity of the Turkish nation should be discussed only on serious platforms, implying that the Motherland Party's convention did not merit serious consideration. In the lengthy release, the military statement argued that "...if political stability cannot be achieved because of personal ambitions, to blame all of the problems on a 'concept of national security' is unreasonable and unjust."[8]

In fact, when Yilmaz used the expression "national security syndrome", he was not referring to a Middle East, Balkan, Caucasus, or Turco-Greek context. Rather, it is evident that the term refers to the struggle for territorial integrity and secularism, which prevents Turkey from fully complying with the EU's criteria for membership. The decision of the December 1999 Helsinki Summit to grant Turkey candidate status placed the onus on Turkey to satisfy the community's criteria with respect to democracy and human rights.[9] It is widely argued that Turkey's bid for EU membership will involve a loss of autonomy and sovereignty that may be incompatible with Turkish national security doctrine. If this is true, it is evident that the nationalist sensitivities of the Turkish political establishment outweigh its Occidentalist outlook.[10] The West is the only community Turkey has tried to join, and Turkish foreign policy has served the nationalist goal of association with Europe. Turkey was welcomed in NATO because of Western security needs; no questions were asked about its internal politics. The EU application, however, has not been as smooth.

Deputy Prime Minister Yilmaz portrayed virtually all negative political, social, and economic issues as stemming from

Turkey's national security concept. This was criticized harshly by the Turkish General Staff, who contended that the national security calculus included threat and risk factors for social, economic, and military parameters.[11] They stressed that the ultimate objective of national security has been to guard a democratic, secular, and unitary republic and to defend the vital interests of the Turkish state and nation. The Commander of the Turkish Land Armed Forces, General Hilmi Ozkok, among others, reiterated the army's responsibility to protect the secular regime. He criticized Yilmaz's views as making the environment more favourable for "Islamists" and "separatists", which might compromise the unity, or even the existence, of the state.[12]

Other voices joined this surprisingly open debate about national security, clearly achieving one of the Deputy Prime Minister's objectives. For clarity, those who joined the discussion can be described in four groups: the pro-military advocates of the status quo; liberals and reformers who agreed with Yilmaz; moderates; and public opinion.[13]

THE PRO-MILITARY CAMP

Ironically, Yilmaz's own coalition partners fell mainly within the conservative pro-military camp. Prime Minister and Democratic Left Party (DSP) Leader Bulent Ecevit, and Deputy Prime Minister and Nationalist Movement Party (MHP) Leader Devlet Bahceli did not back him, the latter saying that this sort of discussion was a waste of time. MHP Deputy Leader Ismail Kose said, "Turkey is a single country, with a single official language, with a single flag...national security cannot be altered. Our policy of security against those who would take up arms against the state in the name of religion or ethnicity will never change."[14]

The Prime Minister publicly declared that he could not comprehend why his junior coalition partner would open such a debate. He criticized Yilmaz, but also (implicitly) the military. Yilmaz was aware of the new security policy document, which concentrated on perception of internal threats, and should have left the matter there. On the other hand, Ecevit was not content with the crude generalization by military leaders that politicians were to blame for Turkey's economic woes. Other leaders also criticized Yilmaz, putting themselves in the pro-military camp. These included True Path Party (DYP) Leader and former Prime Minister Tansu Ciller,

Deputy Leaders Nevfel Sahin and Hayri Kozakcioglu, and former President of the Republic Suleyan Demirel. They argued that his statement should not be taken seriously, that it was subjective and controversial. Sinan Aygun, Chairman of the Ankara Chamber of Trade, agreed that Turkey's globalization adventure had become a process of surrender because of civilian politicians.[15] Former President Suleyman Demirel said that, in 260 national security meetings during the course of his political career, it had never emerged that "Turkey has been harmed because of its national security concept; nor is there a problem with the military."[16]

THE PRO-YILMAZ CAMP

Those who sought democratic change and a shift of power away from the military supported Yilmaz. They agreed that reopening the debate on national security was a prerequisite, but opposed mixing military interests with ideology because ideological challenges had led to numerous military interventions in the past. Freedom of expression in the debate was short-lived. Once the shock effect of Yilmaz's statement wore off, advocates of change were again reluctant to express their views frankly. Those advocating a national security debate were as vigorous as those opposing it. Their reasoning followed the liberal-democratic and human rights discourse, which found support from labour unions, human rights activists, and journalists, all of whom had "suffered" in some way under the national security regime.

The Organization of Human Rights and Solidarity for Oppressed People (Mazlumder) issued a statement supporting Yilmaz. It mentioned that the national security syndrome had been opened for debate for the first time in Turkey, despite the taboo arising from the military's obsession with national security.[17] Mazlumder complained that human rights and basic freedoms were treated as luxuries, while national security policy was dictated from above. Murat Bozlak, leader of the People's Democracy Party (Hadep), stated that only the institutionalization of democracy and social peace would ensure national security.[18] The Liberal Democrat Party leader Besim Tibuk strongly disapproved of the military's monopoly over the management of national security, arguing that "concepts such as freedom and debate might be foreign to them [the military] and that they might misinterpret the Constitution and laws and take it upon themselves to dictate policy."[19]

The General Secretary of the Confederation of Revolutionary Workers Union, Murat Tokmak, complained that national security had been applied arbitrarily and in accordance with the immediate interests and the daily policies of those in Ankara. The Turkish Industrialists' and Businessmen's Association (Tusiad), a wholehearted devotee of EU membership, backed Yilmaz's move to open the "national security" debate. As one might expect, their primary concern was economic success, sustainable under conditions of harmony and stability. For the Tusiad, harmony and stability are synonymous with entering the EU, and they have called for the National Security Council (dominated by the Armed Forces) to adopt EU standards. They have also called for Kurdish education.[20]

At its peak, the columnist Cuneyt Ulsever summarized the debate. The Turkish national security concept is based on an assumption of internal and external enemies, he wrote: "[This] very concept gives a paranoid outlook to the country. Externally, the concept is wary of neighbour states suspected of trying to dig Turkey's grave, of the West trying to weaken or divide her, and of the EU never accepting the membership application. Internally the state is over-suspicious of its own citizens."[21]

MODERATE CAMP

Naturally, some sought a more balanced view. Defence Minister Sabahattin Cakmakoglu of the MHP commented on neither Yilmaz's statement nor the military's, but insisted that all politicians shared a responsibility to deal with the issue amicably; the Turkish General Staff should not feel obliged to issue anti-civilian statements.[22] The leader of the Happiness Party, Recai Kutan, implied that, in democratic countries, politicians, not soldiers, should define the notion of national security. Statements by the Federation of Turkish Labour Unions (Turk-Is) and the Turkish Exporters' Assembly emphasized the economic dimension of national security; Turkey was still struggling with an economic crisis. Turk-Is asserted that "failure to implement social and economic measures in a certain part of the country has resulted in separatist terrorism, ethnic nationalism, and other movements."[23] Continuing the economic theme, the Association of Autonomous Industrialists and Businessmen (Musiad) and the Association of Turkish Young Businessmen (Tugiad) claimed that the debate was untimely and that political stability and confidence were needed to overcome the economic crisis.[24] An intelligence report issued by the National Security Council (NSC) warned that, despite efforts to deal with the growth of regressive faith-based movements (the 28 February process), economic and social problems allowed these groups to continue to recruit new supporters.[25] In short, groups focussing on economic deprivation considered national security principally through the prism of development, and this group tended to be moderate in their approach to the national security syndrome.

PUBLIC OPINION ABOUT THE DEBATE

Despite the engagement of the elites in the debate Yilmaz had initiated, public opinion seemed weak and divided. In an opinion poll at the end of August 2001, four relevant questions were posed to a sample of 1,320 people in eight major provinces. The first question was, "What is the most significant event of this month?" None of the respondents mentioned the debate on the national security syndrome; the most significant events were deemed to be the assassination of a popular businessman (by 29 percent) and the economic crisis (25 percent). The questionnaire also asked, "What is the most significant threat for the near future of our nation?" Again, the respondents seemed oblivious to the security debate, citing the economic crisis (33 percent) and social upheaval (10 percent) as the most significant threats.

Two questions in the August opinion poll concerned the national security debate directly. The first was, "What do you think about Mesut Yilmaz's move to open a debate on national security?" Almost 29 percent considered it positive, half felt it was not necessary, and about 21 percent expressed no views. Assuming that the poll was representative, about a third of the population were pro-Yilmaz, half were pro-military, and the remainder were uncommitted. Another question asked about the "angry outburst" of the military in response to the Yilmaz speech. Almost 36 percent condoned the response, while almost 39 percent condemned the harsh anti-civilian discourse.

The debate subsided towards the end of August when it was reported that Mesut Yilmaz and military members "had a civilized discussion in the NSC meeting." The establishment of Tayyip Edogan's new Justice and Development Party (AKP) replaced the national security syndrome debate as the political topic of the moment.[26]

Yilmaz's speech and the debate that it sparked are illuminating because they expose the complexity of Turkish national security politics. Liberals feel that the subject of national security is taboo, while the pro-military camp treats national security as part of an ideology on which the survival of the state depends.

This brief summary illustrates that there is no general consensus regarding the meaning of the term "national security" in Turkish political and social life. Having described the public debate over the national security syndrome, I will now consider the concept of national security as defined by the state.

The military construes its meaning in terms of threats to official ideology, core national values, and the preservation of sovereignty, territorial integrity, and national autonomy. This stems from its central goal of protecting the regime. For the military, as I argue below, national security is regime security.

The Turkish military has played a considerable role in politics and continues to do so. Military coups in 1960 and 1980 and significant military ultimatums to government in 1971 and 1997 have shaped post-war politics. The military has considerable influence in domestic politics and played a leading role in the formulation and implementation of foreign policy. As Turkey aspires to EU membership, the military is clearly reluctant to relinquish its central role despite declarations of commitment to democratic principles.

Each of the military interventions reflected fears, by military leaders and many civilians, that the survival of the country and its constitution were at stake. The military leadership's self-styled guardianship of the Turkish republic obliges it to intervene if the founding principles of the republic are threatened. In 1960 and 1997, political and religious extremists threatened to take power, and in 1971 and 1980, political strife threatened anarchy and public disorder. Second, the army does not hesitate to intervene if an elected government tries to resort to majority dictatorship (as it appeared to do in 1960). Third, the military will respond if the territorial integrity of the country is threatened by separatism or irredentism; throughout the 1990s, the military controlled the war against the Kurdistan Workers' Party (PKK). Fourth, if civilian governments attempt to curtail its capacity to intervene, the military will step in.[27]

Turkish armed forces have had a guardian role since the beginning of republican rule. As Gareth Jenkins put it, "it sees itself as having an almost sacred duty to protect an indigenous ideology, namely Kemalism."[28] This ideology and the accompanying guardianship ethos of the military are the fundamental norms that have determined the survival of the state. The army's role in society relates to its image as guarantor of the guiding principles of the republic's founder, Mustafa Kemal Ataturk. As a military officer who played a leading role in liberating the country from foreign occupation after the First World War, he led one of history's dramatic political and social reforms. The Ottoman Empire had been ruled by a Sultan, who was also the Caliph, claiming the allegiance of all Muslims. Ataturk created a secular republic whose legitimacy rested on the Western concept of the Turkish nation, but Western nationalism was alien to most of the population in the 1920s. Individual identities were based either on the supranational Islamic *Ummah* or on subnational tribes and local communities. The army was vital as the national institution in which Turkey's new secular identity resided.

The military also plays a dominant role in the National Security Council. Prior to the latest constitutional amendments of October 2001, this institution at the heart of national security planning consisted of the President; the Prime Minister; the Chief of the General Staff; the Ministers of the Interior, National Defence, and Foreign Affairs; and the commanders of the army, navy, air force, and gendarmerie. Since October 2001, the Deputy Prime Ministers and the Minister of Justice have also taken a place in NSC meetings. Depending on the agenda, other ministers and bureaucrats may be invited.

The NSC was established in 1961 to "recommend to the Council of Ministers the necessary basic guidelines regarding the co-ordination and the taking of decisions related to national security."[29] The 1982 Constitution retained the previous composition of the NSC. Article 118 had obliged the Council of Ministers to:

> ...give priority consideration to the decisions of the National Security Council concerning the measures that it deems necessary for the preservation of the existence and independence of the State, the integrity and indivisibility of the country and the peace and security of society.[30]

However, since October 2001, the Council of Ministers no longer has to give priority consideration to the recommendations of the National Security Council.[31] Furthermore, although the civilian members now outnumber those in uniform, it is well-known that military views normally dominate the decisions of the NSC, whose recommendations usually become national policies.[32]

I turn now to the issues, sources, and processes of Turkish national security doctrine. The *National Security Law* of 1983 defines national security in relatively broad terms that could, if necessary, be interpreted to cover the entire policy arena.[33] The Law states that:

> national security means the defense and protection of the state against every kind of external and internal threat to the constitutional order, national existence, unity, and to all interests and contractual rights in the international arena including the political, social, cultural and economic spheres.[34]

More specifically, Article 2b of the *National Security Law* defines national security as:

> the policy which seeks to ensure national security and the achievement of national goals, covering the fundamental principles of the way in which internal, foreign and defence policy is implemented as determined by the Council of Ministers, taking into consideration the opinions expressed by the National Security Council.[35]

Article 3 of the Law, wherein the emphasis is on national unity and integrity and on the values of the Kemalist reforms, specifies nine fundamental duties that determine the necessary measures and objectives in national security management. This is the same law that underpins Ataturk's principle of "Peace at Home, Peace in the World". According to the Law, "with this principle, Turkey determined her national goals to establish peaceful principles, to provide stability and to realize socio-economic development in an environment of peace in her region."[36]

As noted earlier, the two documents that formulate national security priorities and interests are the National Security Policy Document (NSPD) and the White Paper of the Ministry of National Defence. The Council of Ministers is not involved in the preparation of the Policy Document, which identifies the main concerns of national security and sets out the guidelines for security policies. It is produced by the General Staff, the Ministry of Foreign Affairs, and the National Intelligence Organization, under the co-ordination of the NSC General Secretariat. Since the NSPD is not expected to be ratified by Parliament, only the NSC members have full access to it. It is as important as a "secret constitution". It was first drawn up in 1963[37] and is amended when urgent developments change the main national security concerns.

The NSPD was amended in 1997, 1999, 2001, and August 2002. These amendments reflect both foreign threats (Greece, Syria, and

Iraq) and domestic threats (fundamentalism, separatism, and organized crime). In January 1999, the economic crisis, organized crime, and Turkey's poor image were added as new security concerns. In May 2001, the worsening economic crisis and impending social explosion were of deep concern to the monthly NSC meeting. However, a new security document failed to mention the economic crisis as a matter of domestic threat, and the NSC decided to establish a new economic working group under the auspices of the Council. In August 2002, the NSC reported that Greece and Syria no longer represent leading threats to the existence of the Turkish state.[38]

Unlike the NSPD (dubbed the "red booklet"), the National Defence White Paper is unclassified. Like the NSPD, it presents guidelines on security policy to "make peace and stability permanent".[39] Parts three and four describe Turkey's national security and military strategy and provide a brief chronology of Turkish security. This historical précis begins with the establishment of the Supreme Defence Council General Secretariat by decree in 1933. The National Defence Policy of 1949 remained the cornerstone of Turkey's defence policy until the NSC was established in 1961. In the 1960s, Soviet aggression was the dominant security concern for Turkey, as it was for NATO, but this began to change with the political violence of the 1960s. The Armenian Secret Army for the Liberation of Armenia (ASALA) began attacking Turkish diplomats abroad,[40] and the 1974 intervention in Cyprus was punished with an arms embargo. The parameters of national security began to shift.[41]

The ultimate goal of the 1960 and 1971 military interventions was to preserve secularism and the legacy of Ataturk. An earlier draft of the 1961 Constitution stated that "the Menderes government threatened the national existence of the Turkish state."[42] The soft coup of 1971 arose from a tide of domestic violence, fragmentation of political parties, and weak government. After 1971, groups on both the political left and right struggled for radical ideological changes. Sectarian and ethnic conflict arose ominously in several provincial cities. As a result, the military returned to politics in 1980 to restore order and reinstate national political authority. The military council banned political parties and most trade unions existing prior to the coup. During the military rule, 1980 to 1983, new political parties and their preparations for the 1983 elections were monitored by the NSC. The rise of the PKK and other separatist and fundamentalist groups attracted increasing national security attention.[43]

The region most affected by the Kurdish struggle was Southeast Turkey, where martial law was in force from 1984 to 1987. A state of emergency in 13 provinces from 1987 to 1990 was extended to include Batman and Sirnak in 1990. It was lowered to a provisional state of emergency in seven provinces in 2000 and in two more by 2002. Eventually, on 1 December 2002, emergency rule became history when Turkey totally lifted the 15-year practice of emergency rule in southeast Turkey. This marked the end of an era that saw security forces wield sweeping powers against separatist Kurdish rebels. The Ministry of Defence White Paper 2000 describes the PKK as a "terrorist organisation that has adopted the Marxist-Leninist ideology and aims to weaken and divide Turkey with actions based on violence and aims to establish a Marxist Kurdish State in Turkey," and highlights Turkey's successes against it over the last 15 years. The capture of the PKK leader Abdullah Ocalan on 16 February 1999 in Kenya and his subsequent transfer to Turkey were considered a victory of sorts. Armed battles between PKK guerrillas and Turkish forces have diminished since then, and the party changed its name to the Kurdistan Freedom and Democracy Congress (KADEK) in May 2002. The KADEK terminated its operations on 26 October 2003. The Kurdistan People's Congress (Kongra-Gel) was founded on 15 November 2003. The Programme of the Kongra-Gel emphasized democratization as the only true solution for the Kurdish issue.

Democratic freedoms have been curtailed by militarizing the efforts to sustain law and order. From the mid-1990s onwards, there was an enormous increase in the number of files opened and applications to the European Court of Human Rights pertaining to human rights violations in Southeast Turkey. Most of these applications asserted that villages were evacuated and devastated by military forces and that civilians were tortured or raped or disappeared in custody. On several occasions, Turkey agreed to pay large sums of money *ex gratia* to victims of the state of emergency in the region. In 2001, the Court ordered Turkey to pay compensation in 329 cases.[44]

Although the state of emergency is *de jure* a temporary measure, it has *de facto* become permanent. Furthermore, it has created economic, social, and political disparities between regions.[45] Turkey has spent about $7 billion a year on the low-intensity conflict in the Southeast. In 1997, it fielded the largest army in Western Europe, with 820 thousand soldiers, or four percent of the world's armed forces, and 27 percent of Western Europe's.[46] Between four and five percent of the GNP and about 15 percent of the central government's expenditures have been dedicated to military expenditure each year over the last two decades. Meanwhile, the average growth rate of GNP from 1988 to 1999 was just 3.6 percent.[47] Whether the world's sixth-largest army holds back economic development is a question beyond the scope of this chapter, but it is certainly linked to security policy.

Religious fundamentalism became increasingly prominent in Turkish politics in the 1980s and 1990s. Politicization of Islam in Turkey began with Adnan Menderes' Democratic Party and its populist policies in underdeveloped rural areas in the 1950s. The tradition continued with the Justice Party, the National Salvation Party, the National Order Party (in the 1960s and 1970s), the Welfare Party, and the Virtue Party (in the 1980s and 1990s). Today the Justice and Development Party (AKP) represents Islamic constituencies in Parliament. The Saadet Party, a more conservative Islamic political movement, could not pass the national threshold of 10 percent (gained 2.5 percent) to enter the Parliament. In parallel with political Islam, the threat of radical Islamist terrorist groups, such as IBDA-C and *Hizbullah*, rose significantly in the 1980s and 1990s.[48] Fethullah Gulen's *Hizmet cemaati* is a well-organized movement that is based in Turkey but has considerable financial assets as well as schools, television and radio channels, and university organizations in 70 countries around the world. According to military intelligence, Gulen's *Cemaat* has sought to infiltrate government posts in a form of quiet revolution.[49]

By early 2002, most anti-regime activities had been overcome, largely through the implementation of the recommendations from the 28 February Process. Named for the NSC resolutions drafted in 1997, the recommendations were aimed at curbing the growth of political Islam and "anti-state activities" in all spheres of public and political life through changes to the legal framework.[50] In the eyes of the military guardians, even political parties had often been viewed as serious threats to national security. The Constitutional Court outlawed the Welfare Party in January 1998; its successor, the Virtue Party, was also abolished under Article 68 of the 1982 Constitution because of its anti-regime and anti-secular attitudes. Some 15 political parties were outlawed between 1980 and 2001.

In 2002, according to Chief Justice Sabih Kanadoglu, HADEP and Tayyip Erdogan's AKP were both threats to Turkey's secular and republican regime. On 11 March 2003, the Constitutional Court banned HADEP according to Articles 68, 79, 80, 81, and 82 of the Constitution.[51] On the eve of the election on 3 November 2002,

Premier Ecevit stated that "HADEP and AKP would benefit from an early election and that would lead to a regime problem. There have been efforts to represent the separatist movement. We have seen such troubled attempts in the Parliament and similar troubles may be experienced in the future as well."[52] At the time, senior HADEP officials had resigned before the closure to join the Democratic People's Party (DEHAP), a party that was formed in 1997 and largely mirrors HADEP's views. The Constitutional Court is still discussing the case of DEHAP's permanent abolition on charges of aiding the PKK-KADEK and carrying out activities challenging the state.

CONCLUSION

This chapter has described a complex situation in which public order is vigorously contested in the political sphere. The lesson from the debate over the national security syndrome seems to be that the Turkish political establishment needs to set and maintain harmony among key state institutions (including the military, the NSC, and the courts) and civil society organizations (especially political parties). The debate over Yilmaz's accusation demonstrates the ideological constraints and tensions between civil society and the political establishment. When national security is used as a firewall to protect the secular regime, other domestic actors begin to gain strength. Interestingly, these turned out to be Yilmaz's strongest supporters in the debate over the national security syndrome.

The democratic complaint was that the military role of guardian leaves little room for civilian solutions. On the other hand, Kemalists, military guardians, and nationalists fear that democratization would transform the homogenous nation they take to be the foundation of national security. This paradox of Turkish politics has been a subject of concern since the transition to multi-party politics in the 1940s and 1950s. Military involvement has been a substantial factor in democratic consolidation and the emergence of a stable and legitimate political system. The pro-Yilmaz camp attacks this heritage, asserting that the national security syndrome, as part of the official ideology of the state, is a barrier to national development and political liberalization. The incomplete transition to democracy and the exclusion of ethnic and religious groups from politics have given rise to security threats, rather than preventing them. This is clearly evident in the clash of official ideology with political Islam and the Kurdish question.

Turkey's EU candidacy has also been converted into a security concern. The difficult requirements for membership constitute an external shock, since European integration diminishes the autonomy of the state. In this context, Turkey's national security firewall should be reconsidered. If this does not happen, Turkey's EU candidacy itself may come to be seen as a threat to national security in the eyes of the military guardians. On the other hand, the pro-Yilmaz camp sees EU membership as a panacea for economic progress and political liberalization. This tension is clearly evident in the debate over the national security syndrome.

In August 2002 the Turkish Parliament made history in a landmark vote. After a marathon, often raucous, emergency session, lawmakers voted by a show of hands in favour of a package of reforms that abolished the death penalty, gave language and education rights to Kurds, lifted restrictions on right of association and organization, and gave non-Muslim minorities rights over religious property such as churches. Reforms also tightened the regulations governing the police, who are frequently accused of human rights violations. Combined with the lifting of emergency rule in December 2002, it amounted to a serious demonstration of Turkey's commitment to make the changes necessary to qualify for EU membership. "Turkey has taken a giant step on the road to the EU," said Motherland Party (ANAP) leader and Deputy Prime Minister Mesut Yilmaz, who opened the debate on the national security syndrome and whose party drafted the reform package.

A nation-wide poll in May 2002 by the independent Turkish Social and Economic Research Foundation indicated that 64 percent of Turks were in favour of EU membership. It also showed that 90 percent of the Turkish public are unhappy with the functioning of democracy and that EU membership is seen as a democracy project. Seventy-five percent of the Turkish public support the right to speak in one's mother tongue, although Kurdish was not specified.[53] Many Turks accept that the road to Europe is still a long one for a country struggling to overcome a financial crisis that last year halved the value of the lira, slashed more than a million jobs, and sparked the worst recession since 1945. With regard to the democratic reforms, however, it is now likely that at the EU's meeting in December 2004 a date will be set for the start of talks for membership for Turkey.

Critics remain who believe that the reforms will undermine national security. The Nationalist Movement Party (MHP), which had 127 seats in the 550-seat Parliament, fell in the pro-military camp during the national security syndrome debate and was the only party to vote against the entire package in the final vote.

It is difficult to judge, as the pro-Yilmaz camp claims, whether the national security concept is a real obstacle to national development. Rather, there appears to be a trade-off in which the relationship between democratization and national security is a zero-sum game. The political establishment, and the military guardians in particular, assume that some of their political hegemony is lost as ethnic and religious "internal others" gain political access through democratization. The 28 February Process is an example of the resulting efforts at political accommodation.

To conclude, regime security seems to be synonymous with national security in the Turkish case. The national security syndrome, therefore, clashes with democratic culture. Military, political, and civilian elites do not worry much about global technological competition, environmental problems, education, demographics, or even economic dependency. Yet these are the starting points for many of the domestic problems that give rise to threats to the regime. A growing body of scholarship traces the links between national security and national development, and it is now widely understood that narrow military definitions of national security are outmoded. True security demands economic vitality, social justice, and democracy.

NOTES

1.   McNamara, R., *The Essence of Security* (New York: Harper and Row, 1968), 149.
2.   Addressed as part of his *Nutuk* on 30 October 1927.
3.   For the full text of Mesut Yilmaz's speech, see ANAP Leader Mesut Yilmaz's Opening Address at the Motherland Party Congress, 4 August 2001, http://www.anap.org.tr
4.   Author's translation.
5.   Geoffrey Legro, cited in T. Farrell, "Transnational Norms and Military Development: Constructing Ireland's Professional Army," *European Journal of International Affairs*, vol. 7, no. 1 (2001): 82.
6.   The year 1980 provides a good benchmark for the military assuming power: a new constitution was drafted under the supervision of the military, and thus the former socio-political coalition crumbled. For a comparative study regarding the new and old division of labour between state elites and the political elites before and after 1980, see M. Heper and A. Evin, eds., *State, Democracy and the Military: Turkey in the 1980s* (Berlin: De Gruyter, 1988).
7.   Cited in J. Yaphe, *Turkey's Year of Living Dangerously*, Institute for Strategic Studies Occasional Papers, no. 155 (Ankara: National Defence University, January 1999).

8. Turkish General Staff's Press Release, Ankara, 7 August 2001, no. 17.

9. The EU Accession Partnership Documents have made it clear that the withdrawal of the military from the political arena is one of the prerequisites for Turkey's accession. For more about Turkey's progress towards accession, see The European Commission, *Regular Report on Turkey's Progress towards Accession* (November 1998, November 1999, November 2000, November 2001).

10. H. Kosebalaban, "Turkey's EU Membership: A Clash of Security Cultures," *Middle East Policy*, vol. IX, no. 2: 130.

11. *Turkish Daily News*, 12 August 2001.

12. This statement was made on 16 August 2001.

13. These categories do not explain political cleavages or interinstitutional and interelite relations in Turkish politics. It is an *ad hoc* typology intended to identify the parties to the debate on the national security syndrome.

14. *Turkish Daily News*, 11 August 2001.

15. *Turkish Daily News*, 9 August 2001.

16. *Turkish Daily News*, 17 August 2001.

17. *Turkish Daily News*, 9 August 2001.

18. Ibid.

19. Ibid.

20. See *"Türkiye' de Demokratiklesme Perspektifleri" ve "AB Kopenhag Siyasal Kriterleri" no.2 : Düsünce Özgürlüsü* (Istanbul: TUSIAD, September 2001).

21. C. Ulsever, "Will Turkey demolish her fundamental taboo? The role of the army," *Turkish Daily News*, 14 August 2001.

22. *Turkish Daily News*, 11 August 2001.

23. Ibid.

24. *Turkish Daily News*, 13 August 2001.

25. *Turkish Daily News*, 10 August 2001.

26. *Turkish Daily News*, 23 August 2001

27. Adapted from S. E. Cornell, "The Military in Turkish Politics: A National and Regional Stabilizer," *Caspian Brief*, no. 21 (October 2001), http://www.cornellcaspian.com/pub2/21_0111_Turkishmilitary.htm

28. G. Jenkins, *Context and Circumstance: The Turkish Military and Politics* (London: Oxford University Press, 2001), 7. For more about the military factor in Turkish politics, see also Heper and Evin, *State, Democracy and the Military*; W. Hale, *Turkish Politics and Military* (London: Routledge, 1994); D. Lerner and R. Robinson, "Swords and Ploughers: The Turkish Army as a Modernizing Force," *World Politics*, vol. 13 (1960-61), 19–44; M. Heper and A. Guney, "The Military and Consolidation of Democracy: The Recent Turkish Experience," *Armed Forces and Society*, vol. 22, no. 4 (2000), 619–642; U. C. Sakallioglu, "The Anatomy of the Turkish Military's Political Autonomy," *Comparative Politics*, vol. 29, no. 2 (1997), 151–168.

29. Article 111 of the 1961 Constitution. All Turkish constitutional texts, from the 19th century on, can be found in S. Kili and S. Gozubuyuk, eds., *Turk Anayasa Metinleri* (Istanbul: Is Bankasi Yayinlari, 2000), 206–207.

30. Article 118 of the 1982 Constitution, 304.

31. Article 118 was amended on 3 October 2001.

32. See A. Makovsky, *Turkey: Constitutional Challenge Rocks Regime* (Washington, DC: The Washington Institute Policy Watch, Occasional Paper Number 482, 28 August 2000).

33. The *National Security Law*, No: 2945, ratified on 9 September 1983. On its interpretation, see Jenkins, *Context and Circumstance,* 46.

34. *National Security Law*, No: 2945.

35. Ibid.
36. *National Security Law*, No: 2945, Article 3.
37. Jenkins, *Context and Circumstance,* 47.
38. Radikal *"Atina ve Sam artik tehdit degil,"* 02 August 2002.
39. The White Paper of the Ministry of National Defence can be found at www.msb.gov.tr.
40. From 1975 to 1982, dozens of Turkish diplomats and installations of Turkish and Western interests had been the target of ASALA's militant activities.
41. M. Boll, "Turkey's New National Security Concept," *Orbis*, Fall 1979: 610-620.
42. See S. Kili, *Turk Anayasa Metinleri, 1924 Tarih ve 491 Sayili Teskilati Esasiye Kanunun Bazi Hukumlerinin Kaldirilmasi ve Bazi Hukumlerin Degistirilmesi Hakkinda Gecici Kanun, K. Ta.* 12.6.1960, 144.
43. The PKK was identified as one of the 30 main terrorist organizations in the world by the US Secretary of State in October 1997 and by the EU in 2002. It was also described in the same way in US State Department "Patterns of Global Terrorism" reports.
44. For detailed statistics of the cases, see *Survey of Activities of the European Human Rights,* issued by the Registrar of the European Court of Human Rights (Strasbourg: 1998, 1999, 2000).
45. 1982 Constitution: Article 119.
46. US Department of State Bureau of Verification and Compliance, *World Military Expenditures and Arms Transfers, with country rankings for 172 countries by variables* (Washington, DC: US Government Printing Office, April 2000), 2–22.
47. Military expenditures statistics are compiled from *The Military Balance* (London: International Institute of Strategic Studies, 1980-2000). Growth-rate statistics are adapted from *The Turkish Economy 2000* (Istanbul: TUSIAD, 22).
48. On Turkish *Hizbullah,* see Human Rights Watch Press Release, *What is Hizbullah?,* 16 February 2000.
49. See also "Irtica Raporu: Kadrolasma Engellendi," *Hurriyet*, 1 February 2002.
50. N. Gunay. *Implementing the February 28 Recommendations: A Scorecard* (Washington, DC: Washington Institute, Research Note: 10 May 2001).
51. See "Kanadoglu: AKP ve HADEP Ulke Butunlugune Tehdit," *Hurriyet*, 1 February 2002.
52. F. Bila, "They are winking at AKP and HADEP," *Milliyet*, 22 July 2002.
53. Findings were released on 28 June 2002 in Ankara.

eight

"We Are Family"
National Metaphors and Popular Opinions of Conscription in Ecuador[1]

Brian R. Selmeski

Twenty-five years ago, Jack Child published the first comprehensive bibliographic review of Latin American geopolitical thinking in English. He noted that although geopolitics was unpopular as an analytical framework for post-World War II scholars in North America and Western Europe, due in part to its close association with Nazi Germany, the model was a thriving and powerful intellectual influence within the region's armed forces. One of the key metaphors Child identified within the literature was the State-as-organism first posited by German geographer Friedrich Ratzel in 1896.[2]

In his subsequent work, Child expanded on the broad influence of geopolitical thinking in domestic and international arenas. In addition to inter-state conflict, he also noted that "geopolitics can provide a rather consistent explanation for schemes of national development, territorial integration, and [peaceful] relations with neighboring states".[3] Leslie Hepple elaborated on the resultant discursive production of Latin America's geopolitically oriented and inspired military, with particular attention to the correlation between "internal health of the organism" metaphors and the development of a National Security Doctrine that helped shape and justify the Southern Cone's dirty wars of the 1970s and '80s.[4]

This paper examines a parallel and interconnected aspect of the geopolitical State-as-organism metaphor: the nation- and state-as-family. Like the internally focussed health metaphor examined by Hepple, the family model illuminates and shapes the relationship between the armed forces and other segments of society. This is an element largely ignored by Child and classic studies of geopolitics. Unlike the adversarial relationship of the health metaphor, in which "physicians" (soldiers) had to "cut out" (kill or disappear) "cancerous cells" (dissidents) so that the organism (State) could thrive, the Ecuadorean model produces social consensus, at least on the surface, and is shared by the metaphor's different actors. In part this reflects the sharply differing roles of the military under each model: Instead of acting as intervening doctors, like their Southern Cone counterparts, Ecuadorean soldiers are cast as "fathers" who must form their "sons" (conscripts) into good men by teaching them crucial character traits and to respect and love their "Mother" (the *Patria*).[5]

RESPECT THY FATHER, LOVE THY MOTHER: LINKING
NATION, STATE, AND CONSCRIPTS THROUGH METAPHOR

Article 188 of the Constitution makes military service mandatory for all Ecuadorean citizens and permanent residents 18 years of age and over.[6] Unlike the situation in many countries in Latin America, where young men are recruited for military service through coercive techniques colloquially known as "club and rope",[7] most conscripts in Ecuador are eager to complete their service. While in theory a national lottery determines which 20,000 young men will be conscripted each year, those who wish to evade service have a wide range of affordable – and frequently exercised – options. Moreover, of the over 800 conscripts I surveyed, more than 31 percent indicated that they had *not* been selected in the draft but had instead presented themselves voluntarily. Nor are conscripts drawn equitably from all socio-economic strata of society in practice. Yet conscription enjoys broader approval within the marginal sectors of society, which provide a disproportionate of recruits, than with the upper and middle classes, who usually avoid military service. I argue that these unusual data can best be understood by examining shared beliefs about the purposes of conscription in Ecuador.

While most outsiders assume that military service emphasizes primarily martial aspects, with its mere eight-week basic training period, conscription does *not* endeavour to make citizens into professional soldiers. In fact, the process is more concerned with transforming recruits socially than militarily.[8] Conscripts and *voluntarios* (volunteers)[9] believe that one of the keys to this conversion is personal formation, the learning of "good customs" or habits, ranging from brushing one's teeth and working hard to being honest and understanding the importance of a job well done.[10] This is, in many ways, a continuation of the "civilizing mission" initiated by the foreign missions contracted in the early 1900s to modernize and professionalize Latin American militaries.[11]

Today, Ecuadorean Army leaders consider personal formation to be the greatest contribution of military training because it extends beyond the individual and has the potential to renovate the whole of society. As one professional soldier noted candidly, "The problem with Ecuador is that we do things mediocre. We are accustomed to doing things the way we want without exerting much effort. In the *cuartel* [garrison][12] we teach these boys how to do things right – how to comply with their duty. This, in turn, contributes to the development of the *Patria*."

Convincing young men to volunteer for conscription and submit to the formation process, however, is complicated. Force alone is insufficient to assure the system's success, as the egregious cases of Peru, Paraguay, and Bolivia reveal.[13] One of the keys to the success of the Ecuadorean Army is its fusing of the formation discourse with the nation- and Army-as-family metaphor. The result is a hegemonic military doctrine that resonates with many conscripts' conscious and subconscious expectations and desires. The result, according to Roseberry, "is not a shared ideology but a common material and meaningful framework for living through, talking about, and acting upon social orders characterized by domination".[14]

Military service is best understood, therefore, as a forum where young men, their parents, professional soldiers, and politicians craft, express, and act upon their distinct but mutually supportive and overlapping beliefs about family, State, and nation. The Army does not aim to make warriors through conscription as much as it seeks to integrate marginal men, forgotten by governmental agencies and previously unworthy of military service, to the State and shape them into useful citizens.[15] Much like the biblical tale of the prodigal son, today these peasants, Indians, and urban poor are being welcomed back into the family.

When the father welcomes his wayward sons back into the national family, he conducts the reunion in his home, the *cuartel*. The Army's home is a well-organized, efficient, orderly, and self-sufficient unit: in Goffman's words, a "total institution".[16] The *cuartel* is structured both materially, with "a place for everything and everything in its place", and socially. Each family member –

father, son, and Mother – has a specific, prescribed role: fathers direct, sons comply, and Mother nurtures and inspires.[17] Formation is carried out by fathers on behalf of the Mother, completing lessons begun at the breast, ensuring that sons respect their Mother, and meting out discipline when the sons falter. Yet formation and discipline, while intimately connected, are often accomplished through radically different approaches.

FATHERS AND SONS – FORMATION AND DISCIPLINE

> When a young citizen reports for his [military] service, the unit commander becomes like his father.
>
> Senior Ecuadorean recruiting official (2002)

Many young Ecuadorean men are drawn to military service by powerful cultural undercurrents, such as the "Rambo factor", named in honor of the muscle-bound soldier extraordinaire and quasi-patron saint of conscripts. Once inside the *cuartel*, recruits are quickly disabused of this romantic daydream by the tasks they are assigned, as well as by the highly regimented and routine nature of daily life. Most of the conscript's responsibilities are menial chores: peeling potatoes, cutting the lawn, mopping the floor. Outside of the *cuartel*, many would even be considered women's duties. Yet inside, with a dearth of women, they are embraced by sons because fathers portray them as an integral part of the formation process. If performing women's work is what one's father demands in order for one to be well-formed – the underlying goal of conscription – most recruits are willing to comply.

Fathers, after all, set the criteria for the sons' integration with the nation-as-family. Conscripts, as sons and students, are required to obey and comply. If they do, they are told, they can overcome their unfortunate conditions of poverty, unemployment, lack of education, and even counterproductive ethnic customs. Yet fathers are not as uniform as one might imagine in administering the formation process.

Commanders differ from one to another in terms of how they set standards, enforce discipline, administer punishment, and interact (or not) with conscripts. While one officer may punish his entire unit for the mistake of one recruit, another may discipline only the conscripts, and yet another may choose to punish the offender individually. Conscripts adapt to the circumstances with surprisingly little resistance, as all commanders are seen as fathers. Just as one cannot choose one's biological father, neither can one select one's commander, or military father. This situation is further compounded by the fact that conscripts have minimal exposure to officers, who exercise broad fatherly authority by virtue of their rank, and extensive contact with enlisted *voluntarios*, or uncles, whose mandate is more circumscribed.[18]

Fathers and uncles also share a common goal: the formation of conscripts into good sons. Sometimes military fathers, like their biological counterparts, feel they have to castigate their sons to achieve desired results "for their own good". More often than not, this punishment is not resented by sons, but instead portrayed as "for our own good". While this is a tempting opportunity to posit a false-consciousness explanation, conscripts themselves rationalized it in the familial framework. Recruits frequently described the threat of, or actual, punishment as a reflection of their father's concern for their formation that will contribute to their long-term success. While they do not always respond as their fathers would like and do recognize abuse when it occurs, recruits are eager to assume the best of their fathers.

Admittedly, discipline is less draconian in the Ecuadorean Army than in other South American militaries. Corporal punishment, prohibited by law since 1883 but widely practiced until recently, is exceptionally rare today. Most discipline in the contemporary *cuartel* is either physical exertion (e.g., running several kilometers around the base in boots, uniform, and helmet while carrying a backpack and rifle) or additional duties (e.g., guard, kitchen).[19] One basic-training commander, upon observing the recruits marching out of step, exploded, "You haven't learned anything! Doing things half-assed is no good! If you don't start paying attention and executing well, we will march until 20:00 every night and on Saturday and Sunday as well!" The conscripts giggled nervously and marched on, trying to impress their father, while silently acknowledging that this was "for their own good".

Sons do, however, have limits to what they consider acceptable discipline (i.e., that which is for our own good) and respond differently when these limits are disregarded. For example, one of the cruelest punishments invented by creative officers and *voluntarios* to inflict maximum pain without violating military regulations is a position known as "the tripod": recruits assume the push-up position, then raise their rumps into the air, rest their heads on the ground, and place their hands behind their backs.

The strain placed on conscripts' necks, the excessive blood flow to their craniums, and the fact that they are resting much of their body weight on their heads, firmly planted in dirt or gravel, combine to make the position one of few truly reviled punishments. Given the brutality of "the tripod", it is reserved for recruits and never administered to *voluntarios*. Even this sadistic punishment is justified by professional soldiers as contributing to formation by "helping conscripts think" as a result of increased blood flow to their brains. Conscripts do not buy this explanation, however, making their response a product of coercion rather than consent.

There is some tension within the family on non-disciplinary issues as well. This is particularly evident in the experiences of peasant and indigenous conscripts, since the behavioural and linguistic norms that govern the formation of sons are drawn from fathers' and uncles' urban, middle-class *mestizo* culture. Many of these cultural foundations are either shared, papered-over by means of the father-son relationship, or overlooked by conscripts fearful of the tripod. Others are more conflictive, problematic, and/or deeply held, forcing conscripts to confront a dilemma: should they emulate their biological father or their metaphorical father? The simple solution put forward by the Army is that one should give up any counterproductive beliefs and practices learned from one's biological father. Conscripts do not always put this standard into practice as easily as the Army expects, though, demonstrating both the naïveté of military officials and the power of culture to compel us to act against our own best interest.

For example, when a conscript answered a *voluntario's* question in the meek and quiet voice typical of a peasant or highland Indian, he was berated to "speak like a man!". After he failed to comply a second time, he was ordered to run 50 meters to the middle of the parade field and answer "like a man". When he still did not adopt the loud, brash tone of "a man", he was made to do pushups, calling out the number of repetitions he had completed. Not surprisingly, the sergeant could not hear him because he wasn't "speaking manly enough", so he made the conscript start over again, taunting him to "shout like a man".

The idea of shouting for no apparent reason was so foreign to this recruit that he suffered repeated humiliation because of his inability to meet the *voluntario's* expectations. In North American terms, the *voluntario* was trying to turn a mild-mannered Midwesterner into a loud, aggressive, confrontational, perhaps even obnoxious New Yorker. Not everyone wants to, or is able to, speak like a New Yorker – or urban, middle-class *mestizo* – as this may contradict the very essence of his culture. Moreover, if he were somehow able to adopt this foreign behavioural model, the conversion would require him to betray his roots. Yet this is precisely what Indian recruits must do if they wish to exploit conscription's opportunity to redefine their relationship with the State. Those *indígenas* [aboriginals] who do speak and act "appropriately" are held up as role models for Indian and non-Indian recruits alike; those who do not are roundly chastised and humiliated.[20]

The national family, just like many flesh-and-blood families, is replete with tensions and conflicts, in this case between strong-minded fathers and noncompliant sons.[21] Although these clashes strain the metaphorical family, they do not necessarily destroy it, just as parent-child flare-ups in literal families rarely threaten the family structure. This conscript did not run away (desert) after the encounter – desertion rates are remarkably low in the Ecuadorean Army – nor do most adolescents in broader society. In both cases, I suggest, when sons feel that they are being treated fairly, that their parents share and assist them in reaching their goals and are not abusive, they are loath to abandon their families and homes.[22] What is more, while sons may have tense relations with their disciplinarian fathers, the metaphorical Mother plays a very different role, giving rise to a distinctive parent-child relationship.

MOTHERS AND SONS – LOVE AND DUTY

The *Patria* does not exist without the love of Her sons.

Sign at the entrance of the basic training centre (1999)

Both metaphorical and biological mothers are portrayed by the Army as givers of life, the providers of continuity, shelter, and sustenance. In one officer's words, mothers are "half-human, half-divine". Without mothers, the family would not be perpetuated; there would be no new fathers to serve the Mother, nor sons to assist through conscription. Nor would conscripts arrive at the *cuartel* with the foundation of culture and habits that forms the core concerns of the formation process. Although formation is believed to be fully achieved only through the intervention of military fathers, biological mothers initiate the process by nurturing their children from a young age.[23] The centrality of mothers to the military mission helps explain the presence of the otherwise incongruous statue of a nursing woman at the entrance to the Riobamba *cuartel*.

Despite the absence of conscripts' literal mothers from the *cuartel*, their *Patria* is omnipresent in daily praxis and discourse. These two aspects fuse during the weekly Civic Moment, when the entire brigade comes together to hear inspirational speeches, sing patriotic songs, and recognize each others' achievements. The *Patria's* symbols – particularly the flag, national anthem, and seal (*escudo*), as well as the men and arms of the military itself – are placed at centre-stage during these rituals. These reminders of conscripts' Mother are inescapable in the *cuartel*.

In the words of one Army officer addressing the troops during a Civic Moment, the *Patria*, like biological mothers, is seen as:

> ...tireless, diligent in her duty – the care for her children – in providing the first caresses of affection to her beloved child, who she delivers to the world and society with exceptional happiness and whose first steps she tutors, whose tears she dries, wounds she heals, fears she assuages, who she comforts in difficult times and whose aspirations she encourages.

The *Patria* fulfils similar metaphorical roles. She assuages the pain of past territorial losses by fixing the blame and inspiring citizens to right the wrong someday, comforts by providing a sense of origin and continuity, and unites by making individuals part of a nation.

In return, sons have a duty to their mothers. They should honour, defend, and give back to the *Patria* by completing their military service and vigorously expressing their patriotism. It is not enough to feel civic pride; one must express it by displaying the national flag on appropriate holidays and singing the national anthem enthusiastically. Sons should also work diligently in a profession that will contribute to the country's economic development. All of these actions are intended to please the Mother; hence, the same officer concluded his speech by insisting that soldiers should:

> ...honour our mother as she deserves, for we are testimony to her enormous sacrifice that produced what we are today. Our flower of gratitude should exude a delicate perfume to enchant our mother. While alive we should shower her with the happiness that is within the realm of each of her children because it is so delightful to be a loving son and cause her to smile and make our mothers happy.

Pleasing conscripts' biological mothers and making them proud provides yet another important impetus to young men's decisions to serve. In countries where military service is voluntary, popular perception is that mothers naturally protest the State/ armed forces "stealing" their sons for conscription, but Ecuadorian recruits suggest otherwise. Ninety-nine percent reported their mothers as "not opposed" to their military service. Moreover, 63 percent reported their mothers to be "proud" of their sons' decision to serve, and almost half described their mothers as "happy" about their actions. Even Indian women, whom outsiders would expect to be most suspicious of the military, were generally supportive of their sons' decisions. Those I interviewed admitted to being apprehensive at first, but after visiting their sons on Sunday afternoons, they too began describing the Army in fatherly terms. The family metaphor, it seems, is accepted by not only conscripts and soldiers, nor is it limited to the *cuartel*; it resonates with different ethnic groups and generations in civil society as well.

The importance of biological mothers and their sons' desire to please them is exploited by national conscription authorities. In one recent television commercial promoting conscription, a young man leaves home in jeans and returns in uniform to his jubilant family. His first interaction is with his mother, who hugs and kisses him while a disembodied voice confesses, "I have never seen my mother so proud as the day I reported for my military service." His father shakes the young man's hand, and siblings congratulate the conscript as well, but the focus of the interaction is the mother-son dyad. He served for her, and she is proud and hugs him fervently.

The nature of sons' relationships with their biological and metaphorical mothers changes over time but does not end when they finish their period of active service. This is seen most clearly in the *juramento a la bandera* (swearing to the flag) ritual that marks the end of conscripts' service.[24] Each recruit comes forward individually and kneels before his commanding officer, who lifts the flag, the symbol of the Mother, with his saber. The son then professes his intention to defend the Mother, "Her flag, the constitution, and the laws of the Republic, the integrity of the nation and not abandon those who command you in times of war or preparation for the same" at the top of his lungs – "like a man" – for all to hear. In doing so, sons join their fathers by assuming their duty to protect the Mother they dearly love.

Never has a conscript not sworn. If duty and making one's literal mother proud were not enough motivation, the rejoinder from the officer administering the oath likely alleviates any doubt. "If you so swear," they are told, "the *Patria* will reward you; otherwise, She shall condemn you." For a conscript, to forsake this duty would be to fail both his biological mother and the *Patria*.

The consequences of not swearing could put the *Patria*'s very future at risk, for as the sign that begins this section proclaims, She "does not exist without the love of Her sons."

PROTECTING OUR BELOVED MOTHER: POPULAR OPINIONS OF DEFENCE, THE ARMY AND MILITARY SERVICE

Pardon me, mother of mine, if my absence causes you to suffer;
Pardon me, mother of mine, if I must die for my *Patria*;
Your womb gave me life, you soothed me with love;
Now that I am a grown man, I am the eternal defender of you, mother, and of my *Patria*.

lyrics from the popular marching cadence "Madre Mía" (1996)

The Ecuadorean military constructs the *Patria* not only as the metaphorical Mother but also as a virtuous woman, pacific, patient, and persistent, who has consistently been victimized. Conscripts are taught that the once proud and expansive Kingdom of Quito, colonial Audience of Quito, and subsequent Republic of Ecuador – all linked in the national-origin myth as developmental stages of the *Patria* – have been reduced to a fraction of their original size and grandeur by aggressive and expansionist neighbours. While Colombia and Brazil have wronged the *Patria*, Peru is cast as the primary perpetrator.

Peruvian aggression has not only challenged the territorial integrity of Ecuador but, in the military's prose, "dismembered", "penetrated", and "violated" her. The Mother has been raped repeatedly by the expansionist-minded Peruvians, beginning with the Conquest and continuing through the War of Cenepa, the 1995 border conflict. The armed forces alone have preserved Her life in war, although like Inca general Rumiñahui, who razed Quito and slaughtered the temple virgins rather than let them fall into the hands of Spanish conquistadors, they have been able only to minimize the pain inflicted by invaders, not prevent it. By portraying past incursions as assaults on the Mother through the use of powerful and graphic organic and sexual terms, the military transforms national pride from an abstract and ephemeral concept into a tangible and compelling motivation in peacetime.[25]

After all, according to the Army, it is the obligation of all citizens to defend virtuous women, especially their literal and figurative mothers.[26] As the lyrics of the marching cadence in the above epigraph romantically suggest, participating in national defence may result in a conscript's death. This may cause one's biological mother to experience emotional pain, but is better than losing one's *Patria* or permitting Her integrity as a virtuous woman to be desecrated yet again. Although conscripts, their parents, *voluntarios,* and officers may all have slightly different ideas of what it means to be a "good son", none dispute the obligation of sons to defend their mothers when they are threatened.

As sons of the *Patria,* former conscripts also play an integral role in national defence, bound by this unwritten but transcendental filial duty: as long as the Mother is alive, they are Her sons and are obliged to protect Her. Nor can officers and *voluntarios* alone ensure the *Patria's* longevity, they insist; they are too few and are inadequately funded, equipped, and armed. Only a unified nation can overcome these deficits, making the integration of Indians to the State via conscription a paramount concern for military planners. In practice, the Army-father, as the *Patria's* husband, bears the primary responsibility for Her defence but must enlist the day-to-day help of their sons through conscription and call on ex-conscripts (emancipated sons) when the Mother is in imminent danger.

Although conscripts are obliged to help their fathers defend the *Patria* after completing their service, they never become the father's equal. Once sons return to civilian life, the Army continues to define and perceive them according to their former status as conscripts, the lowliest of military personnel. While a conscript ranks higher in the figurative "Order of the *Patria*" than his peers who evaded service – an altar boy to the officer/high-priest – he is not, and never will be, a professional soldier. Conscripts are, therefore, sons who will never become fathers in the military sense, even after completing their service or reaching 55 years of age and being permanently discharged from the Reserves. Regardless of their chronological age, unless they become *voluntarios,* conscripts and ex-conscripts are destined to be perpetual bachelors, in military terms.[27] Yet, in the eyes of Ecuadorean conscripts, it is better to be an old, single, and well-formed son – a male spinster – than a bastard or an orphan, unacknowledged and forsaken by the State/Army and the nation/*Patria.*

This is not always the case, as the Cuban joke below reveals:

The school inspector asks Pepito:
Who is your mother? – The *Patria,* inspector.
And your father? – Fidel, inspector.
And what do you want to be when you grow up, Pepito? – An orphan, inspector.

Apart from reinforcing the parental roles of the *Patria* as mother and uniformed Head of State as father, the joke suggests that the family metaphor is difficult to escape. Pepito rejects the Cuban *Patria* and president but does not, perhaps cannot, discard the metaphor. In fact, the idea of a national family still resonates with him and delineates the nature of his relationship to the State and nation. Pepito cannot ignore the "fact" that he is a son of the *Patria* and Army; the best he can do is wish they were no longer part of the same family. That he does not consider himself parentless and repudiate the family metaphor completely is indicative of both the coercive power of the State-system ("a palpable nexus of practice and institutional structure centred in government", personified by the school inspector) and the consensual appeal of the nation-State idea in the abstract when couched in kinship terms.[28] That Pepito recognizes his Mother and father despite rejecting them reveals the degree to which the family metaphor is taken for granted as part of the "real world" and shapes even resistance to the concepts and forms that facilitate rule.

The joke provides clear testimony that the nation-as-family metaphor is not an exclusively Ecuadorean phenomenon. It also reminds us that, powerful and broadly shared though it may be, the metaphor is not always successful in motivating citizens to love, respect, and serve their nation-State.[29] Families, literal or figurative, are sometimes dysfunctional, conflictive, and discordant. Pepito rejects his family, wishing they either would not recognize him or would die prematurely. (If they died of old age, he would not be an orphan but, rather, would assume the father's role, a possibility as impossible for a Cuban youth as for an Ecuadorean conscript.) If the inspector were not present, he might even assume the radical and socially reprehensible position of advocating the killing of his Mother or father or both: patricide, matricide, or both.

Yet I suspect that Pepito, like most Latin American revolutionaries, would *not* advocate the death of the Mother, only the father.[30] In part, this speaks to the powerful attributes and beliefs associated with motherhood, like those described during the Civic Moment. Whereas the Mother-nation is seen as a passive and well-intentioned influence, the father-State is associated with active rule and, therefore, with oppression and abuse. To kill off the Mother would be to destroy the family's inspiration, glue, and touchstone, disconnecting sons, like Pepito, from their brothers and sisters, leaving them alone and detached from society. To kill just the father, on the other hand, would permit the son to introduce his

Mother to a new father-State, theoretically reestablishing unity and harmony in the family unit. Revolution does not, after all, generally have anarchical goals; it does not seek to topple the State as much as to replace the current state-system with a new one, more favourable to insurrectionists' interests and beliefs. I suggest that these beliefs are not only ideological in nature but also cultural. Stepfathers must not only be from the "right party" but also have the "right qualities".

What makes the Ecuadorean case exceptional, then, is not the presence of the family metaphor, but how it gains cultural capital through understandings, sometimes shared, sometimes negotiated, of each member's appropriate role. The nation- and State-as-family construct derives its power to compel young men into service from two sources. First, like other metaphors, it is flexible and can "slide from one form of the metaphor to another".[31] Accordingly, the metaphor is alternatively used to describe Ecuador's *past* – as a family feud between "Ecuadorean" and "Peruvian" brothers, both heirs to the Inca Empire; *present* – where fathers and sons protect the Mother; and *future* – reinforcing the role of women and childbirth as central to the perpetuation of the family. Second, it is shared in large part by legislators who write conscription laws, soldiers who execute them, the young men who comply, and the mothers, fathers, and girlfriends who encourage service. Regardless of differences of interpretation, the metaphor is broad and common enough to be adopted by a large portion of Ecuadorean society. This has reified the nation- and State-as-family metaphor, converting it to a taken-for-granted assumption. In the process, it has facilitated the Ecuadorean Army's drafting of young men and helped conscription garner favourable public opinion despite its demise elsewhere in Latin America[32] and its categorization as anachronistic in the developed world.

NOTES

1. This work is based on 22 months of ethnographic and archival fieldwork made possible by funding from the Social Science Research Council (SSRC), the Fulbright Commission of Ecuador, and Syracuse University, as well as by the institutional support of the *Ministerio de Defensa Nacional, Facultad Latinoamericana de Ciencias Sociales* (FLACSO) and the *Pontificia Universidad Católica del Ecuador* (PUCE).

2. Jack Child, "Geopolitical Thinking in Latin America," *Latin American Research Review* 14:3 (1979): 89–111.

3. Jack Child, *Geopolitics and Conflict in South America: Quarrels among neighbors* (New York: Praeger Press, 1985), 5.

4. Leslie W. Hepple, "Metaphor, Geopolitical Discourse, and the Military in South America." in *Writing Worlds: Discourse, text, and metaphor in the representation of landscape,* Trevor J. Barnes and James S. Duncan, eds. (London: Routledge, 1992).

5. *Patria* can be roughly translated as "nation" in the sense of patrimony, culture, and identity, rather than simply territory. However, I strenuously object to the alternative definition as "fatherland" for reasons explicated in this chapter. Unless otherwise specified, for the purposes of this chapter, the terms "family", "father", "son", and "Mother" denote metaphorical (i.e. family = nation, father = professional soldiers, son = conscript, and Mother = *Patria*), rather than literal, kinship roles.

6. Although the Ecuadorean Constitution of 1998 considers military service to be the obligation of all citizens and residents, regardless of sex, the armed forces draft only men.

7. Peter M. Beattie, *The Tribute of Blood: Army, honor, race, and nation in Brazil, 1864-1945* (Durham: Duke University Press, 2001).

8. Although the content of the processes are radically different, this emphasis on acculturation rather than military training strongly resembles the case of the U.S. Marine Corps' boot camp. Thomas E. Ricks, *Making the Corps* (New York: Simon and Schuster, 1997).

9. *Voluntarios* are professional soldiers, all of whom have completed their obligatory military service and subsequently enlisted (volunteered).

10. Officers, enlisted men, and conscripts all distinguish personal formation from intellectual formation (i.e., schooling), physical formation (i.e., fitness), and military formation (i.e., training). While the processes are interrelated, personal formation is the bedrock of the four, the indispensable component to achieve complete formation.

11. Brian Loveman, *For la Patria: Politics and the armed forces in Latin America* (Wilmington: Scholarly Resources, 1999) and Frederick M. Nunn, *Yesterday's Soldiers: European military professionalism in South America, 1890-1940* (Lincoln: University of Nebraska Press, 1983).

12. *Cuartel,* while literally translated as barracks, is better understood as a military base or garrison.

13. Rodolfo Elías, Gabriela Walter, and Juan Carlos Yuste, *Pensando en la baja ... la experiencia del servicio militar obligatorio desde los adolescentes y sus familias* (Asunción: Servicio Paz y Justicia, 1999); Ronald Gamarra, *Servicio Militar en el Perú: historia, crítica y reforma legal* (Lima: Instituto de Defensa Legal, 2000); Juan Ramón Quintana Taborga, *Soldados y ciudadanos: un estudio crítico sobre el servicio militar obligatorio en Bolivia* (La Paz: Programa de Investigación Estratégica en Bolivia, 1998).

14. William Roseberry, "Hegemony and the Language of Contention," in *Everyday Forms of State Formation: Regulation and the negotiation of rule in modern Mexico,* Gilbert M. Joseph and Daniel Nugent, eds. (Durham: Duke University Press, 1994), 361.

15. Theoretical wranglings as to the nature of the State aside [see, for example, Philip Abrams, "Notes on the Difficulty of Studying the State," *Journal of Historical Sociology* 1(1) (1988): 58–89], in practice the military appears to conscripts not as an arm of the State but as the State itself: the Army created the *Patria,* polices, defends, and develops Her, and presumably always will. This view is shaped by the armed forces, is shared by much of the population – skeptical of electoral politics, tired of corruption, and fondly recalling enlightened military juntas of the past – and is strongly reinforced in conscripts' minds through daily life in the *cuartel.* See Loveman, *For la Patria.*

16. Erving Goffman, *Asylums: Essays on the social situation of mental patients and other inmates* (Garden City: Anchor Books, 1961).

17. Daughters are conspicuously absent from the *cuartel* both literally, because it is a male-dominated space, and metaphorically, because they are being groomed to be mothers, a process carried out in their natal homes. Only recently have women been admitted to the military academy in small numbers, a change that will likely necessitate a revision of the Army's family metaphor in the coming years.

18. Anthropological literature has long pointed to the importance of fathers' and mothers' brothers (i.e., paternal and maternal uncles, in North American kinship terms) in the shaping of youth in so called "primitive societies". A.R. Radcliffe-Brown, "The Mother's Brother in South Africa," in *Structure and Function in Primitive Society* (New York: The Free Press, 1965 [1952]), 15-31. While I take inspiration from this and related works, my emphasis in this chapter is on the symbolic meanings rather than functional roles assigned to fathers, mothers, and uncles.

19. While it is tempting to assume that conscripts rationalize to themselves that punishment in the form of physical exertion makes them stronger, they consistently stated that it was more important for conscripts to be capable than to be physically strong. Capability, in this sense, is a proxy for personal formation, as one can be competent in their worldview only if one is well-formed.

20. Not all indigenous conscripts are treated poorly nor equally in Ecuador; native Amazonian recruits are often lauded in the *cuartel* for their supposedly innate martial prowess, and certain highland Indian groups, such as the Otavalos, are *a priori* held up as exemplars of "good Indians". On Amazonian soldiers, see Brian R. Selmeski, "Warriors and Citizens: Racial stereotypes and military roles of Ecuadorean indigenous conscripts", in *Military Service in Latin America: Processes and tendencies*, Oscar Guillermo Vásquez Bermejo, ed. (Lima: American Friends Service Committee, 2001), 77-91. Regarding "good Indians", see Brian R. Selmeski, *Multicultural Citizens, Monocultural Men: Indians and national defence in Ecuador* (Ph.D. dissertation: Syracuse University, forthcoming).

21. Though such conflicts are absent from the *cuartel*, one could imagine a similar reaction from the Army-Father to a daughter of the *Patria* eager to explore her sexuality out of wedlock, as this act would violate his notion of appropriate behavior.

22. I suggest that the fear of retribution should they be caught and anxiety over how they would survive without their family structure, while related, are less compelling factors in discouraging desertion.

23. Mothers are not condemned for their sons turning out unformed because the Army recognizes the inability of mothers to control the influences to which their adolescent sons are subject once they leave the natal home to work or study in the city.

24. Elsewhere I have described in greater detail how the role of women – metaphorical or real – in this ritual and the *Entrega de Armas* (Bestowal of Arms) ceremony, when conscripts receive their rifles from their biological mothers, is paramount in the construction of military notions of masculinity in Ecuador. Brian R. Selmeski, "Making a Few New Men: Masculinity and conscription in Ecuador," *Proceedings of the XXIV International Congress of the Latin American Studies Association* (2003).

25. Hepple, *Metaphor, Geopolitical Discourse, and the Military*.

26. Loveman, *For la Patria*.

27. This characterization applies to Indian and non-Indian recruits alike and may help to further explain the high percentage of conscripts who want to

become *voluntarios* once they complete their service, despite their high rate of ineligibility, which results from inadequate education.

28.   Abrams, "Notes on the Difficulty of Studying the State".

29.   My use of "nation-State" is an attempt to juxtapose and conjoin the two elements linguistically in much the same way that Quechua creates the word couple by uniting "man" and "woman" into a new word; it should not be construed as reproducing the fallacy of the unitary nation-state frequently seen in uncritical political theory.

30.   A quick review of the revolutionary writings of José Martí, Ernesto "Che" Guevara, Father Camilo Torres, Emiliano Zapata, and others reveals a persistent concern with the *Patria* despite a rejection of the governments and armies of the day.

31.   Hepple, *Metaphor, Geopolitical Discourse, and the Military*, 141.

32.   Francisco Rojas Aravena and Rodrigo Araya Dujisin, *Visión comparada del Servicio Militar en las Américas* (Santiago: FLACSO-Chile, 2001).

nine

EUROMIL and the Citizen in Uniform

Donna Winslow

The initial impetus to integration in the direction of a postnational society is not provided by the substratum of a supposed "European people" but by the communicative network of a European-wide political public sphere embedded in a shared political culture. The latter is founded on a civil society composed of interest groups, nongovernmental organizations, and citizen initiatives and movements.[1]

This study began with a conversation over dinner with Mr. Bauke Snoep, Vice President and future President of European Organization of Military Associations (EUROMIL). We were attending a conference on civilian control of the military in The Hague where I was hoping to find funding for a project on the European Defence Identity. As we will see later, the European Defence Identity is still in an early developmental phase. However, in discussion with Mr. Snoep, I realized that this idea was growing and that organizations such as EUROMIL are contributing to its construction. I went on to develop a research project in discussion with the Brussels office and the Board of EUROMIL, and the actual work began in June 2001.[2]

The goal of the research was to examine the identity of the organization and how this identity promotes cultural interoperability[3] in EUROMIL, which is an umbrella non-government organization founded in 1972, comprising a variety of military associations from 19 European countries. My belief was that EUROMIL would contain elements that promote a common identity and structured difference.[4] This tension between commonality and difference is explored in another more detailed report, which was presented to the EUROMIL Presidium.

This chapter discusses what binds the members of EUROMIL together – a shared military culture and a vision of the "citizen in uniform". It goes on to look at how EUROMIL builds the notion of the European citizen in uniform. Even though many interviewees told me that the EU soldier does not yet exist, the fact of their participation in EUROMIL contributes to the development of the EU concept. This also creates commonality in EUROMIL. As one interviewee remarked, "Being part of EUROMIL is an important way to build up the idea of the EU soldier. Like the EU citizen, it doesn't exist yet. Part of the way to build up the EU idea is to stay in EUROMIL."

A SHARED MILITARY CULTURE

According to Soeters and Recht,[5] although there are differences in national military cultures, there are enough indications to prove the existence of an overarching international military culture. In their study of military schools around the world, they observed that military cadets show significant cultural differences based on national affiliation, but they also demonstrate the shared values of a worldwide military culture. As one interviewee observed, "The uniform is an international culture. Militaries share something above national differences."

Similarly, Elron and Ben-Ari describe how military troops often arrive for service in multinational forces sharing what may be called a common military culture.[6] This military culture is distinctive, has clear boundaries, and can be considered as separate within the larger society. The military's distinctive culture sets it apart from the rest of civilian society. This separateness is emphasized by the military's distinctive dress (uniform, distinctive badges, headgear, etc.), language (unique terminology, acronyms, etc.), and an emphasis upon ceremony and tradition (parades, mess dinners, etc.). This culture is also marked by hierarchy (expressed by ranking and the chain of command) and by its corporate character.

Military culture is also one of the reasons that EUROMIL members are able to work together. One interviewee said, "EUROMIL is the best way of working together in the EU, particularly because we are military people and we have lots in common. We know each other, speak a common military language." Another found this shared military culture to be one of EUROMIL's greatest strengths; it allows the members of EUROMIL to overcome national differences. "Sometimes it is difficult to understand different realities of each country, but we have the link of military to create common ground."

The particularity of military culture and military life is one of the reasons that EUROMIL argues that it is uniquely positioned to defend the special interests of the "citizen in uniform". EUROMIL tells us that, due to their special conditions of service (i.e., unlimited liability), military members are not just civil servants; they are something else. "More and more EU military are willing to be treated as equal to civil servants, but we are specific and need specific treatment." "We need to represent the military as unique and as a special group with professional interests." Thus, EUROMIL sees itself as representing a special interest group. "EUROMIL is able to lobby for the specific need of the military as compared to the ETUC [European Trade Union Confederation] which represents public servants – they can't concentrate on the special needs of soldiers."

Even though militaries are something "different", EUROMIL believes that they should not be denied the democratic right of participation in organizational matters that private businesses and public service associations have enjoyed for a considerable time. Servicemen and -women should be allowed to raise issues of professional concern with the leadership in government and the ministry of defence without being restricted to using the chain of command. Unfortunately, this is the precise reason why some militaries wish to deny their membership the right to association: it might undermine the chain of command. EUROMIL believes this to be an unfounded argument. In the view of one interviewee, "The biggest challenge for EUROMIL is to transmit to others in uniform (especially higher levels) that democracy is not dangerous and that associations can contribute to justice and discipline." Similarly, a senior commander from the Netherlands (where there is a long tradition of association) said, "Associations just make us more responsible as commanders. They are useful."

THE CITIZEN IN UNIFORM

According to Delanty, citizenship has become a major new area of debate in the social sciences:

> The growing literature on this topic and journals such as *Citizenship Studies* have highlighted challenges such as technology, ecology, the media, group rights, and consumerism for a new king of citizenship beyond nationality... Citizenship today has become a major site of battles over identity and demands for recognition of group difference.[7]

EUROMIL also asks for recognition of group difference: that is, recognition of the military as a special professional category: "the citizen in uniform". As mentioned earlier, EUROMIL argues that the military should have the same rights as other citizens, *but* it is also something different because it is a unique professional group. "We accept that soldiers can be asked to do more than the ordinary citizen – even make the ultimate sacrifice. But there should be no barrier to equal treatment."

EUROMIL's concept of "the citizen in uniform" comes from the leadership philosophy of the German armed forces – the "inner leadership" model. "The Germans call it 'state citizen in uniform'. You fight for values of your state. 'State citizen' implies high respect for constitution and respect for the dignity of man." The philosophy of inner leadership was a cornerstone of the democratization process in the German armed forces after World War II.

> The [inner leadership] model describes a responsible citizen, who on the one hand enjoys his/her democratic constitutional rights intensely yet responsibly, but who, on the other hand, unrestrictedly accepts his/her professional obligations as a soldier being prepared to protect also human rights with his/her life if worst comes to worst.[8]

All the member associations from EUROMIL consider themselves committed to the principle of "citizen in uniform"; however, they experience it differently, depending upon their history. For example, the Northern associations have a long tradition of association and have acquired many citizenship rights over the years. In Denmark, members of the military can stand for political office; in Finland, they have the right to strike; and in Germany, they can make public statements while in uniform. I was told by some of these Northern associations that the concept is not used in the same way as in countries where soldiers have no rights because soldiers are simply *not* considered different from other citizens. In interviews with representatives from the associations in the Southern/Mediterranean countries where military members have few rights, the concept of the citizen in uniform was used to talk about rights that soldiers "should" have in order to "reach" the same level of freedom as any other normal citizen. As one Southerner put it, "We are defenders of democracy. How can we defend democracy when we don't have it?"

The former Warsaw Pact associations see the concept from yet another perspective. I was told, "In former times, armies were very separate from citizens. They were a world apart." Thus, the idea of a citizen in uniform is a new one. "We were just out of massive restructuring; we were not conscious of our rights." EUROMIL has played an important role in spreading the idea of the citizen in uniform, and this concept can play a role in the democratization of former Eastern Bloc militaries in the same way as it did in Germany after the war. "When we encountered EUROMIL for the first time, we were not clear about what the citizen in uniform meant. But through contacts with old EUROMIL members, we learned what it means and why EUROMIL exists. All citizens should be equal under the constitution." This is important because, according to some prominent political scientists, the core principle of democracy is citizenship.[9]

EUROMIL argues that members of the armed forces, who have asked to protect and defend the rights and freedoms of their fellow citizens, should be entitled to enjoy and exercise those same rights and freedoms. One of these fundamental rights is the right to freedom of association. EUROMIL uses international laws and agreements to support the argument. For example, Article 20 of the Universal Declaration of Human Rights of the United Nations says: "Everyone has the right to form and to join trade associations for the protections of his or her interests." This is interesting, since human rights are based upon an ethical and legal concept of the individual, while citizenship rights are based on a political and legal understanding of the individual. They share a legal conception of the individual, but differ with respect to universality. Human rights are basic ethical rights that all individuals enjoy by virtue of their common humanity, whereas citizenship rights are specific to a particular political community.[10] In this case, EUROMIL defines the community as a military community.

> EUROMIL asserts the right to found associations or unions in order to represent social interests (the right of association) and advocates that this practice of association activity has to be anchored in the appropriate national and international laws, agreements and conventions for all servicemen. The right of association includes the right to found an association, the freedom to belong to it and the possibility of this association and of its members, to

act in and on behalf of the association. The right to represent social interests in an association includes not only the right and freedom of founding associations with the aim of safeguarding and furthering the economic and labor conditions, but also of joining this association and acting in and on behalf of the association. It includes also the freedom of setting up the statutes and articles of the association. The right of association can be restricted by a prohibition to strike for political reasons. The member associations from EUROMIL resign from the right to strike.[11]

The European Citizen in Uniform

EUROMIL makes reference not only to the "citizen in uniform" but to the *European* citizen in uniform. "Being in EUROMIL means we can participate in constructing the citizen in uniform in Europe. We are building a project and creating common levels of rights and standards across Europe." This is important, particularly for the Northern associations, since they fear that an EU army will be reduced to the lowest common denominator. "There is a chance that we will go down to a lower level in the EU in order to be at the same level as other national forces." "The EU might choose the lowest common denominator; therefore, it is important that we help raise standards in other countries." Soldiers who carry out the same duties should not be subject to different terms of employment and social protection. It is, therefore, necessary to harmonize soldiers' rights at the level of the European Union.

In EUROMIL, the broader image of the European citizen in uniform consists of four elements:

- a free person in the spirit of a constitution based on the principle of liberty;
- a serviceman or -woman who is ready for action to defend and enforce human rights;
- a responsible citizen of Europe; and
- a responsible citizen who plays an active part in shaping his or her conditions of service in the armed forces.[12]

This means that European states have the obligation to ensure that comprehensive welfare provisions are in place for their armed forces and their families and to guarantee servicemen and -women the right to freedom of association. "Europe means people coming together for a common purpose, and it also means there should be no difference in the application of rights to soldiers of different countries."

EUROMIL believes that members of the armed forces should be allowed to help build a better Europe, and certainly, citizenship is an important European issue:

> Among the debates concerning the building of the EU, the issue of European citizenship ranks high. Indeed, attempts to delineate the definition as well as the content of such a citizenship have given birth to a large literature, questioning its actuality, feasibility or even its very desirability. But which jurists, political scientists or sociologists argue heatedly over the hopes or threats such a new (level of) citizenship would entail, much of these discussions tend to stay at a theoretical and/or normative level, and only a few authors refer to actual practices in which citizens would be involved and which would foster new affiliations or sets of references, or to policies and discourses produced by European institutions on this issue.[13]

According to Bellier and Wilson, European institutions help build or reinforce new social and political categories, such as citizens.[14] Delanty's book, *Citizenship in a Global Age*, considers the concept of cosmopolitan citizenship, which is not restricted by the geographical boundaries associated with the nation state (hence its associations with globalization).[15] Cosmopolitan citizens, according to this increasingly influential position, are citizens of the world community, not of any particular state, because cosmopolitan community is replacing national community. And although EUROMIL simply wants citizens in uniform to have the same rights as their fellow national citizens, the current focus on multinational peace operations and the discussion about the European army mean that the rights of soldiers in overseas missions could derive from something other than a nation state, e.g., the UN or the EU, which would guarantee their rights to certain basic working conditions, the right to representation, etc.

NATIONAL CITIZENS

In the current context, however, EU citizens are first and foremost national citizens. This means that the "citizen in uniform" is first a member of national military and governed by the policies of the national government he or she serves. The EU leaves to the member states the determination of how EU policy applies to their military. As Lt. General Rainer Shuwirth[16] has noted in relation to the EU security and defence project, the European Parliament has no responsibility and no decision-making power.

> The influence of the EU into the member states' national military organiza-
> tions is limited. One can try to convey a message through the military repre-
> sentatives to the national military but the effect of the information is up to
> the member states as long as security policy is organized intergovern-
> mentally.[17]

The result is a very heterogeneous set of standards and conditions of work for military members across Europe. For example,
some EU countries, such as the Netherlands and Germany, have a
long tradition of association within the military. Others, such as
Ireland and Portugal, have only recently recognized this right, and
in still others, such as Spain, France, and Italy, the military are
still denied this fundamental right. These differences become particularly salient when members of European militaries find
themselves working side by side in an international peace operation with different rights, pay scales, levels of protection for family
members, health and safety standards, etc. "We are having to work
in the same missions, yet soldiers in same missions have different
rights. This is a big issue and not easy. EUROMIL has to be more
active in establishing common rights. It creates problems when
soldiers have different rights."

EUROMIL protests against these differences, saying, "joint missions, joint rights",[18] and seeks to redress these imbalances between
European militaries. In order to accomplish this, the member associations of EUROMIL tap into supranational "repertoires" of
human rights, citizenship, and democracy (particularly the right
of association and "frames" on European-ness) to formulate,
strengthen, and legitimize their own national goals and struggles.
Member associations draw on alliances formed through EUROMIL
and on EUROMIL itself to lobby for better representation and quality of life in their own countries. In this way, they are forging
alliances based on profession across national boundaries. Eighty
percent of the Eastern associations that I interviewed told me that
they found bilateral partnerships forged through EUROMIL very
important. These partnerships were formed with Northern associations in order to assist the Eastern associations in getting
established. For example, the Danish associations gave computers
and photocopy machines to the Czechs and paid Latvia's membership dues in EUROMIL for two years. The Netherlands has a
partnership with Hungary, Germany with Russia, and so on. Assistance is not only financial; it is shared experience. As one interviewee

said, "EUROMIL consists of very experienced members, and we can benefit from that experience."

All the interviewees from the Southern countries told me they joined EUROMIL to obtain support in their national struggles. They see EUROMIL as a "big brother" they can call in for assistance or as an "umbrella" offering protection. "We wanted an international defence of our interests." "It was the only place where we could receive support and exert outside pressure." "It is important that we are not alone, and EUROMIL offers aid and support in the background." "We feel safe fighting for our rights because, being in EUROMIL, we feel we won't be persecuted. A big brother is watching over us." Eastern associations see EUROMIL as a helper. A member from an Eastern association commented that it was helpful to be able to use examples from EU countries when lobbying national authorities.

And EUROMIL has helped many of its members in their national struggles. For example, when the Italians took a complaint to the European Court of Human Rights, EUROMIL supplied the legal expertise, so the Italians only had to pay to file the complaint. The President actively intervened on behalf of the Bulgarian association to influence politicians and the Ministry of Defence. More than ten years ago, two Irish representatives attended a Presidium meeting in Denmark. They met with the Managing Board of EUROMIL and told them about the bad situation in Ireland. As one member of the Managing Board at that time told me, "We said, okay: we will ask the Presidium for full support, such as help with lawyers and family support if they are arrested, and we told them that they could use phone and fax at our hotel to inform Ireland of EUROMIL's decision. They left with a feeling of support." This initial contact was followed up with a EUROMIL visit to Ireland, which focussed public attention and press coverage on the situation.

Similarly, when I attended the Presidium meeting in Seville in April 2002, it was clear that it brought a lot of public attention to the struggle of the Spanish associations to get the right of association. Numerous newspaper articles highlighted the situation, and a television program described how the Spanish Ministry of Defence had indicated that active personnel were prohibited from joining an association even though the Spanish constitution recognizes this right. Clearly, holding the EUROMIL Presidium in Spain assisted the Spanish associations in their struggle.

CONCLUSIONS: GLOBAL CITIZENS

As early as 1893, the famous sociologist, Emile Durkheim, in his book *The Division of Labor in Society,* foresaw a differentiated modern society, which requires generalized values and a form of solidarity based upon cooperation among social groups, such as occupation and professional organizations and education. Such a generalized value system would be based not on the values of a particular social group but on shared civic values. It is clear that Durkheim had in mind a republican conception of citizenship and believed that the cohesion of a society rests on citizenship as more than a civic bond but also as a part of identity. In this case, EUROMIL's discourse and actions on behalf of the citizens in uniform are contributing to the creation of an identity category that was formerly "military" but now encompasses something more – the citizen.

EUROMIL tells us that the goals of unification, harmonization, and integration – key processes in the context of Europe-building – require an alteration in the core areas that used to be defined within the frame of nation states. In particular, national defence policies and the determination of EU states to keep control over defence run counter to the fostering of common forms of EU identity and affiliation. They may even subvert efforts to build a common European defence force.

We can see that, as a result of the Maastricht Treaty, EU citizens already have a number of rights – to move and reside freely within the territory of the Community, to vote and be eligible to stand for election to local and EU parliaments, etc. Such a series of rights creates new opportunities for direct relationships between these individual citizens and Europe, bypassing the national level.[19] Thus the questions arise: Will EU soldiers be true EU citizens? Will they be members of a polity beyond their individual state? Will they be entitled to social rights that may be distinct from or in addition to those allowed in member states, but that will integrate them into a larger community of "European soldiers"? Or will EU citizenship remain fragmented, with certain rights for groups of Europeans, but not all Europeans?

EUROMIL's demand for the recognition of citizens in uniform and the determination of EU-wide policies of the right to representation, conditions of service, and so on feeds the EU debate on differentialism or universalism. Will European practices of citizenship modify relationships to territory? Will such changes flow from citizenship being based on a different set of references, such as access to rights flowing from universal human rights or from residence, and no longer from belonging to a national community?[20]

This is of particular interest for the military, which is traditionally tied to the defence of a national territory. Is the recent development of a common European Strategic Defence Initiative the beginning of a European Defence Force? What does a European Army of the future mean for the traditional relationship between army and defence of national territory? Will the EU then constitute a "nation" to be defended? These are debates that EUROMIL is uniquely positioned to deal with.

At this moment, however, the European soldier seems a distant reality. I was told, "What we have now are national soldiers, and the EU is under construction." "EU soldiers are artificial soldiers. There is no EU nation, no EU defence policy, thus no EU soldier." Nevertheless, EUROMIL members see it as a future reality, and being in EUROMIL is contributing to that reality. "Being part of EUROMIL is an important way to build up the idea of the EU soldier. Like the EU citizen, it doesn't exist yet, but part of the way to build up the EU idea is to stay in EUROMIL." "The EU soldier is not yet a reality; it is a vision."

The future of the European soldier, and perhaps EUROMIL, will depend upon the developing role of the EU as a solitary entity in defence matters. In many ways, EUROMIL is ahead of its time. The consciousness of a common belonging, which its members share, is the belonging to a larger family of the military. EUROMIL members constitute a community of interest based upon their profession. Moreover, in their reference to the citizen in uniform, they open the door to affirming themselves as members not only of the community of military service members but of the Community of Europe.

NOTES

1. J. Habermas, *The Inclusion of the Other: Studies in Political Theory* (Cambridge, MA: MIT Press, 1998), 153.
2. The information presented here is a product of my observations during the EUROMIL meetings I have attended, what I have read about the organization, and particularly the comments found in semi-structured interviews I carried out with EUROMIL members. Unattributed quotations throughout the chapter are from those interviews.

3.   Culture represents the behaviour patterns or style of an organization that members are automatically encouraged to follow. Culture shapes action by supplying some of the ultimate aims or values of an organization, and actors modify their behaviour to achieve those ends. It establishes a set of ideal standards and expectations that members are supposed to follow. It is important to remember that culture is not only a set of values, or ethos; it is also the customary style used in organizing action. For a detailed discussion of both army and military cultures, see D. J. Winslow, *Army Culture,* a Report Prepared for the US Army Research Institute (Alexandria, VA, 2000); D. J. Winslow and C. Dandeker, "Challenges to Military Culture from Living in the 21st Century", in *Governance in the 21st Century,* Transactions of the Royal Society of Canada, Series VI, Volume X, D. Hayne, ed. (Toronto: University of Toronto Press, 1999), 195–218.

4.   See D. J. Winslow, *The Canadian Airborne Regiment in Somalia. A Socio-Cultural Inquiry.* (Ottawa: Minister of Public Works and Government Services Canada,1997); D. J. Winslow, *Bacovici, A Report on the Breakdown of Discipline in CANBAT II.* A Report Prepared for the Chief of the Defence Staff (Ottawa: 1998); D. J. Winslow, "The Role of Culture in the Breakdown of Discipline during Peace Operations," *Canadian Review of Sociology and Anthropology Special Issue: Organizational Crisis,* no. 35.3 (August 1998): 345–368; D.J. Winslow, "Misplaced Loyalties: The Role of Military in Culture in the Breakdown of Discipline in Two Peace Operations," in *The Human in Command: Exploring the Modern Military Experience,* C. McCann and R. Pigeau, eds. (New York: Kluwer Academic/Plenum Publishers, 2000), 293–310; D. J. Winslow, "NGOs and the Military," *Militaire Spectator,* vol. 10 (2000): 525–534.

5.   J. Soeters and R. Recht, "Culture and Discipline in Military Academies: An International Comparison," *Journal of Political and Military Sociology,* vol. 26, no. 2 (1998): 169–189.

6.   E. Elron, B. Shamir, and E. Ben-Ari, "Why Don't They Fight Each Other? Cultural Diversity and Operational Unity in Multinational Forces," *Armed Forces and Society,* vol. 26 (1999): 73–97

7.   D. Delanty, *Citizenship in a Global Age. Society, Culture, Politics* (Buckingham: Open University Press, 2000), xiii.

8.   EUROMIL, "EUROMIL Today" (Brussels: EUROMIL, mimeo, January 2002): 6.

9.   G. O'Donnell and P. Schmitter, *Transitions from Authoritarian Rule: Tentative Conclusions about Uncertain Democracies* (Baltimore: John Hopkins University Press, 1986).

10. Delanty, *Citizenship in a Global Age,* xiii.

11. EUROMIL, "EUROMIL in Brief" (Brussels: EUROMIL, mimeo, March 2002): 1.

12. EUROMIL, "EUROMIL Policy Objectives" (Brussels: EUROMIL, mimeo, October 2000): 8

13. I. Neveu, "European Citizenship, Citizens of Europe and European Citizens," in *An Anthropology of the European Union: Building, Imagining and Experiencing the New Europe,* I. Bellier and T. M. Wilson, eds. (Oxford: Berg, 2000), 119.

14. I. Bellier and T.M. Wilson, "Building, Imagining and Experiencing Europe: Institutions and Identities in the European Union," in Bellier and Wilson, *An Anthropology of the European Union,* 15.

15. Delanty, *Citizenship in a Global Age,* xiii.

16. Lt. General Rainer Shuwirth is Director General EU Military Staff and former Commanding General IV Corps, Germany.

17. Lt. General Rainer Shuwirth, in a debate following his presentation "The Military Dimension of European Security and Defence Policy," to the 4th

International Forum of EUROMIL, entitled "Armed Forces in Europe – Political Mission and Social Dimension," Brussels, 12 November 2001.

18. Lead Association Multinationality, Draft position paper "Joint Mission – Joint Rights? Social conditions during missions abroad" (Berlin: mimeo, 15 November 2001), 2.
19. Neveu, "European Citizenship," 124.
20. Ibid., 133

ten

Education, Public Perception and the Profession of Arms in Canada

John Scott Cowan

This chapter addresses the enduring myth that members of the armed forces do not need to be well educated. It traces the origins of this myth and the reasons for its persistence, in the context of the changing nature of the work done by the armed forces and the criteria for regarding practitioners of that work as members of a profession. From an examination of current trends in the education of officers and non-commissioned members, the chapter draws conclusions about both the value of education in the Canadian Forces and the professional nature of the career for which it prepares them and keeps them effective.

EDUCATION FOR CANADIAN OFFICERS, PAST AND PRESENT

The first steps towards an educated profession of arms in Canada began with the recognition in the early 1870s of the inadequacy of the three-month "short" course in the artillery schools, and the subsequent decision of the Mackenzie government in 1874 to found the Royal Military College of Canada. It opened in 1876 with a four-year post-secondary program that has proven hugely durable; in fact, it was very much like a modern undergraduate degree. It was not, however, until the report of Major General Roger

Rowley in 1969 that a clear public case was made for the systematic education of the entire officer corps. The implementation of Rowley's vision was long delayed, but recent defence ministers and most of the senior leadership in the Canadian Forces (CF) since the late 1990s have been strong supporters of education, both for the officer corps and for non-commissioned members (NCMs) of the CF. The Withers Report on future directions for RMC in 1998 and two recent reports from the Special Advisor to the CDS (Officership 2020 and NCM 2020) all added momentum, and in 2001, the overall conduct of education and professional development for the CF was accorded to the newly created Canadian Defence Academy (CDA), 33 years after Rowley advocated such a structure.

Thus, despite the best efforts of earlier champions, broad acceptance within the Canadian Forces of the critical role of education for the profession of arms is relatively recent. Indeed, one might argue that it is not yet here, as there is a good bit of lip service to the concept still and there are persistent pockets of cynicism. But on the whole, there is an acceptance that effectiveness requires plenty of education. Even prior to the creation of the CDA, there were some tangible manifestations of this new view. Amongst these were the decision to have a degreed officer corps, and a series of developments related to RMC. From having no outreach programs eight years ago, RMC now provides distance and part-time education at the undergraduate or graduate level to over 3,000 members of the CF who are not at its campus in Kingston. Together with the Canadian Forces College (CFC) at Toronto, it has built a new accredited professional graduate degree, the Master of Defence Studies (MDS) on the platform of the Command and Staff Course at CFC, and 42 persons were awarded this degree in 2002. The new undergraduate core curriculum at RMC recommended in the Withers Report has been implemented; the first class on that curriculum is now about to enter fourth year. Under that scheme, all undergraduates, whether their degree is in literature or mechanical engineering, or in any other field, must show a minimum competence in subjects essential for officership: specifically, psychology, ethics, leadership, Canadian history, military history, political science, civics and law, international affairs, cross-cultural relations, logic, math, information technology, physics, chemistry, English, and French. You may note that, from time to time, RMC is criticized by the uninformed for not providing a liberal education.

Furthermore, in 2002 RMC awarded about 450 degrees, of which 135 were master's or PhD degrees, roughly one for every two undergraduate degrees. About 80% of the new graduate degrees for the officer corps were taken through RMC.

WHY ATTITUDES HAVE RECENTLY CHANGED

Why is this awakening occurring now? The idea is not new. H. G. Wells described the history of humankind as "a race between education and catastrophe". Of late, this has become especially vivid for the modern profession of arms, so the timing of the shift in attitude is not surprising.

On the one hand, the public in the developed world have come to view any significant failure of judgement within the profession of arms as a genuine catastrophe. We would be profoundly unwise to dismiss this as merely anti-military bias and an appetite for scandal. While those factors may amplify that perception, the perception itself is inextricably tied to the rising attention to human rights issues in both foreign and domestic policy throughout the developed world.

On the other hand, the remarkable acceleration of technological change and the growth of knowledge have the potential to be a vast multiplier of the effectiveness of numerically small forces. This is part of RMA, the Revolution in Military Affairs. But it also amplifies the need for complexity of thought and maturity of judgement to avert catastrophe and drives that requirement further down the chain of command than ever before.

Traditionally, of course, in the CF, some education was viewed as "nice to have", but training was viewed as the real way to prevent catastrophe. Today, when an officer may be called upon to be a skilled leader, a technical expert, a diplomat, a warrior, and even an interpreter and an aid expert, all at once, there is no doubt that good training is not enough. Skills are not enough. The job calls for judgment, that odd distillate of education, the thing that is left when the memorized facts have either fled or been smoothed into a point of view, the thing that cannot be taught directly, but that must be learned. Without the mature judgment that flows from education, we fall back on reflexes, which are damned fine things for handling known challenges, but are manifestly unreliable in the face of new ones. And there will be new ones.

THE STEREOTYPE VS. THE FACTS

In Canada, however, there is still an outdated but widespread stereotype of long standing that equates military service with lack of education. On the whole, the general public is not much exposed to the CF, and hence few Canadians realize that military personnel learn in more breadth outside their first discipline than do most others in society, hold more varied jobs, and change jobs and take courses more often. In fact, the educational programs designed for military personnel are predicated on the certainty that they will need to know more than others in society. Indeed, the knowledge base for the profession of arms spans most of human knowledge.

These facts would surprise much of the public, many of whom still think that military training is as portrayed traditionally in film. They largely do not imagine that the preparation of an officer touches on most of the disciplines found in a modern university, and that this preparation extends throughout an entire career.

But a unique and dangerous aspect of the anti-education myth and stereotype is not that many in the broader society believe it to be so, but that some within the Canadian Forces still view too much education as an impediment.

During the interviews conducted for the Withers report of 1998 on the future directions of RMC, we heard some remarks from serving officers about too much education. Some argued for just-in-time education; they clearly misunderstood what education was for.

Even the comments from our own masters and doctoral students used to echo the established mythology that getting a graduate degree interrupted or slowed an officer's career, while getting a graduate degree and teaching at RMC derailed one's career completely.

Well, old biases die hard, but, evidently they are dying. In the past year we gave master's degrees to a Brigadier General and to a Major General. Two years ago, one RMC faculty member left to take command of the Third Battalion, Princess Patricia's Canadian Light Infantry, and has now returned from Afghanistan. One year ago an RMC history professor who is an infantry officer with a PhD took command of the First Battalion, Royal Canadian Regiment, at Petawawa. One of the best engineering officers on our faculty, who got a PhD at Queen's but never expected to be promoted above captain, was promoted to major and allowed to remain at RMC.

This is evidence of a profound sea-change and proof that learning, even at the master's or PhD level, is becoming accepted and valued in the Canadian Forces. That is by itself a sort of Revolution in Military Affairs. Some imagine that the RMA is purely a technological revolution, a revolution of devices. The real RMA is knowledge and ideas. And that is the RMA that will value education in the practitioner of the profession.

EDUCATION AND THE PERCEPTION OF PROFESSIONALISM

These changes will also affect how the broader society sees the profession of arms. That is because the broader society links the concept of a profession with advanced education.

Within the defence community, we speak easily of the profession of arms. But there are portions of Canadian society who find the term curious or pretentious and who have trouble accepting that it is a profession. What could possibly make them think it is not?

True professions have three incontrovertible characteristics. First, a profession must be, at least to some extent, self-regulating. In addition, its existence must serve a higher public purpose. And, finally, its practitioners must know, use, and codify a definable and substantial body of higher knowledge relevant to that profession.

I have written elsewhere about the first two. On the question of self-regulation, the profession of arms does better than any other profession. I would be happy to defend that position anywhere.

On the test of higher public purpose, the CF exist to protect national sovereignty, to maintain conditions for peace, order, and good government, and to make certain that the interests of Canada and of Canadians are not trampled by aggressors. There are those who doubt the higher public purpose, but they represent the portion of the public who are "whistling past the graveyard", which is to say those who are so naïve or so terrified that they can't bring themselves to admit that the post-Cold War world is not a safe place and haven't realized that today, geography is no shield and neutrality is no exemption.

That brings us to the last criterion. Since one of the measures of a profession is that its members must know, use, and codify a definable and substantial body of higher knowledge relevant to that profession, the anti-education myth reinforces the reluctance of the broader public to accept the profession of arms as a true profession. It is the new attitude to knowledge in the CF that will eventually erase all doubt in the public mind that there exists a definable and substantial body of higher knowledge relevant to the profession of arms. The doubt shouldn't have been there, of course. In no other profession do the members spend such a large fraction of their careers receiving professionally relevant education and training. The existence of RMC, CFC, the Canadian Forces Leadership Institute, the published work in the *Canadian Military Journal*, the activities of the Canadian Defence Academy, the schools for the Military Occupational Categories, the very existence of the Officer General Specification, and all of the establishments working on doctrine or higher competencies are all part of that effort. I suspect that even the severest critics of the Canadian Forces don't really doubt the existence of the relevant body of knowledge, because they're constantly going on about how they think we haven't disseminated it well enough.

So it may be that education and higher knowledge are the preventatives for catastrophe, the soul of military renewal, and the final confirmation to the Canadian public that there is a genuine profession of arms in Canada.

Contributors

Douglas Bland holds the Chair in Defence Management Queen's University School of Policy Studies in Kingston, Ontario.

John Cowan is the Principal of the Royal Military College of Canada in Kingston, Ontario.

Ulrich vom Hagen is a sociologist employed by the German Armed Forces.

Deborah Heifetz-Yahav is an anthropologist at the University of Tel Aviv, Israel.

Tami Jacoby teaches political science at the University of Manitoba, In Winnipeg, Canada.

Thorstan Kodalle is an analyst for the German Armed Forces.

David Last teaches political science at the Royal Military College of Canada, in Kingston.

David Morse is the Commandant of the Canadian Defence Academy in Kingston, Ontario.

Alan Okros is director of the Canadian Forces Leadership Institute in Kingston

Franklin Pinch is the president of the Canadian section of the Inter-University Seminar on Armed Forces and Society, and researches at the Canadian Forces Leadership Institute in Kingston, Ontario.

Leena Parmar is a sociologist at Rajasthan University in Jaipur, India.

Brian Selmeski is an anthropologist at the Canadian Forces Leadership Institute in Kingston, Ontario.

Donna Winslow holds the Chair in Anthropology at the Amsterdam Free University in the Netherlands

Gökhan Yücel is a PhD candidate at St. Anthony's College, Oxford, in the United Kingdom.

Queen's Policy Studies
Recent Publications

The Queen's Policy Studies Series is dedicated to the exploration of major policy issues that confront governments in Canada and other western nations. McGill-Queen's University Press is the exclusive world representative and distributor of books in the series.

School of Policy Studies

Clusters in a Cold Climate: Innovation Dynamics in a Diverse Economy, David A. Wolfe and Matthew Lucas (eds.), 2004   Paper ISBN 1-55339-038-5 Cloth 1-55339-039-3

Canada Without Armed Forces? Douglas L. Bland (ed.), 2004
Paper ISBN 1-55339-036-9 Cloth 1-55339-037-7

Campaigns for International Security: Canada's Defence Policy at the Turn of the Century,
Douglas L. Bland and Sean M. Maloney, 2004
Paper ISBN 0-88911-962-7 Cloth 0-88911-964-3

Understanding Innovation in Canadian Industry, Fred Gault (ed.), 2003
Paper ISBN 1-55339-030-X Cloth ISBN 1-55339-031-8

Delicate Dances: Public Policy and the Nonprofit Sector, Kathy L. Brock (ed.), 2003
Paper ISBN 0-88911-953-8 Cloth ISBN 0-88911-955-4

Beyond the National Divide: Regional Dimensions of Industrial Relations, Mark Thompson,
Joseph B. Rose and Anthony E. Smith (eds.), 2003
Paper ISBN 0-88911-963-5 Cloth ISBN 0-88911-965-1

The Nonprofit Sector in Interesting Times: Case Studies in a Changing Sector,
Kathy L. Brock and Keith G. Banting (eds.), 2003
Paper ISBN 0-88911-941-4 Cloth ISBN 0-88911-943-0

Clusters Old and New: The Transition to a Knowledge Economy in Canada's Regions,
David A. Wolfe (ed.), 2003   Paper ISBN 0-88911-959-7 Cloth ISBN 0-88911-961-9

The e-Connected World: Risks and Opportunities, Stephen Coleman (ed.), 2003
Paper ISBN 0-88911-945-7 Cloth ISBN 0-88911-947-3

Knowledge, Clusters and Regional Innovation: Economic Development in Canada, J. Adam
Holbrook and David A. Wolfe (eds.), 2002
Paper ISBN 0-88911-919-8 Cloth ISBN 0-88911-917-1

Lessons of Everyday Law/Le droit du quotidien, Roderick Alexander Macdonald, 2002
Paper ISBN 0-88911-915-5 Cloth ISBN 0-88911-913-9

*Improving Connections Between Governments and Nonprofit and Voluntary Organizations:
Public Policy and the Third Sector,* Kathy L. Brock (ed.), 2002
Paper ISBN 0-88911-899-X Cloth ISBN 0-88911-907-4

Institute of Intergovernmental Relations

Canada: The State of the Federation 2002, vol. 16, *Reconsidering the Institutions of Canadian Federalism*, J. Peter Meekison, Hamish Telford and Harvey Lazar (eds.), 2004
Paper ISBN 1-55339-009-1 Cloth ISBN 1-55339-008-3

Federalism and Labour Market Policy: Comparing Different Governance and Employment Strategies, Alain Noël (ed.), 2004
Paper ISBN 1-55339-006-7 Cloth ISBN 1-55339-007-5

The Impact of Global and Regional Integration on Federal Systems: A Comparative Analysis, Harvey Lazar, Hamish Telford and Ronald L. Watts (eds.), 2003
Paper ISBN 1-55339-002-4 Cloth ISBN 1-55339-003-2

Canada: The State of the Federation 2001, vol. 15, *Canadian Political Culture(s) in Transition*, Hamish Telford and Harvey Lazar (eds.), 2002
Paper ISBN 0-88911-863-9 Cloth ISBN 0-88911-851-5

Federalism, Democracy and Disability Policy in Canada, Alan Puttee (ed.), 2002
Paper ISBN 0-88911-855-8 Cloth ISBN 1-55339-001-6, ISBN 0-88911-845-0 (set)

Comparaison des régimes fédéraux, 2ᵉ éd., Ronald L. Watts, 2002
ISBN 1-55339-005-9

John Deutsch Institute for the Study of Economic Policy

The 2003 Federal Budget: Conflicting Tensions, Charles M. Beach and Thomas A. Wilson (eds.), 2004   Paper ISBN 0-88911-958-9 Cloth ISBN 0-88911-956-2

Canadian Immigration Policy for the 21st Century, Charles M. Beach, Alan G. Green and Jeffrey G. Reitz (eds.), 2003   Paper ISBN 0-88911-954-6 Cloth ISBN 0-88911-952-X

Framing Financial Structure in an Information Environment, Thomas J. Courchene and Edwin H. Neave (eds.), Policy Forum Series no. 38, 2003
Paper ISBN 0-88911-950-3 Cloth ISBN 0-88911-948-1

Towards Evidence-Based Policy for Canadian Education/Vers des politiques canadiennes d'éducation fondées sur la recherche, Patrice de Broucker and/et Arthur Sweetman (eds./dirs.), 2002 Paper ISBN 0-88911-946-5 Cloth ISBN 0-88911-944-9

Money, Markets and Mobility: Celebrating the Ideas of Robert A. Mundell, Nobel Laureate in Economic Sciences, Thomas J. Courchene (ed.), 2002
Paper ISBN 0-88911-820-5 Cloth ISBN 0-88911-818-3

Available from: McGill-Queen's University Press
c/o Georgetown Terminal Warehouses
34 Armstrong Avenue
Georgetown, Ontario L7G 4R9
Tel: (877) 864-8477
Fax: (877) 864-4272
E-mail: orders@gtwcanada.com